Marou Izumo and Claire Maree

LOVE UPON THE CHOPPING BOARD

Marou Izumo
and
Claire Maree

(Translated by Claire Maree)

Spinifex Press Pty Ltd
504 Queensberry Street
North Melbourne, Vic. 3051
Australia
women@spinifexpress.com.au
http://www.spinifexpress.com.au

First published by Spinifex Press 2000
© Copyright Marou Izumo on chapters 1, 3, 4, 6, 7, 9, 10, 12, 13, 15,
17 2000
© Copyright Claire Maree on chapters 2, 5, 8, 11, 14, 16 2000
© Copyright on Translation Claire Maree 2000
© Copyright on typesetting and layout: Spinifex Press Pty Ltd 2000

Edited by Janet Mackenzie
Typeset in Goudy and Palatino by Palmer Higgs Pty Ltd
Cover design by Deb Snibson

Made and printed in Australia by Australian Print Group

National Library of Australia
Cataloguing-in-Publication data:
Izumo, Marou, 1951– .
    Love upon the chopping board.
    ISBN 1 875559 82 5.
    1. Izumo, Marou, 1951– . 2. Maree, Claire, 1968– . 3.
Lesbians – Biography. 4. Lesbians – Japan. 5. Feminism –
Japan. 6. Feminists – Biography. I. Maree, Claire, 1968– .
II. Title.

306.76630952

This project has been assisted by the Commonwealth Government
through the Australia Council, its arts funding and advisory body.

For all girls and women who, to the question

"Why do you love the same sex?"

can only answer,

"I love because I do."

AUTHORS' NOTES

The title of this book is taken from a word-play on the Japanese proverb *manaita no ue no koi*; literally "the carp upon the chopping board". This proverb expresses situations where there is nothing but to leave it all up to fate. In Japanese, *koi* (carp) and *koi* (love, passion) are homonyms.

All Japanese names appearing in this book are written according to Japanese language conventions where the family name precedes the first name.

ACKNOWLEDGEMENTS

Chapters 1, 3, 4, 6 and 7 are translated adaptations of work originally appearing as:
Izumo, Marou. 1993. *Manaita no ue no koi* (Love Upon the Chopping Board) Tokyo: Takarajimasha.

Chapter 7 is an edited version of work which appeared as:
Izumo, Marou, and Maree, Claire (Claire Maree trans.). 1997. "Watashi, Otambi, Dyke", in Susan Hawthorne, Cathie Dunsford, Susan Sayer (eds) *Car Maintenance, Explosives and Love and Other Contemporary Lesbian Writings*. Melbourne: Spinifex Press.

Chapter 6 is indebted to information contained in the following texts:
Hiratsuka, Raichō. 1971. *Genshi, josei wa taiyō de atta* (In the beginning, women were the sun). Tokyo: Ōtsuki Shoten.
Hiratsuka, Raichō. 1994 (1955). *Watashi no aruita michi* (The path I've walked). Tokyo: Nihon Tosho Senta.
Komashaku, Kimi. 1994. *Yoshiya Nobuko: Kakure Feminisuto*. (Yoshiya Nobuko: closeted feminist). Tokyo: Riburopōto.
Sawabe, Hitomi. 1990. *Yuriko dasubidanya* (Goodbye Yuriko). Tokyo: Bungei Shunjūsha.
Tanabe, Seiko. 1999. *Yume Haruka Yoshiya Nobuko*, Vol. II (Distant dreams Yoshiya Nobuko). Tokyo: Asahi Shinbunsha.

CONTENTS

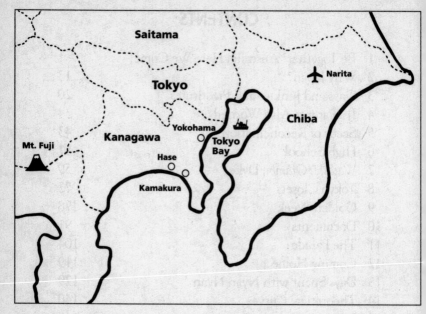

Tokyo and surrounding area

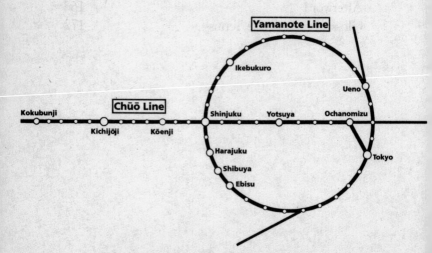

Tokyo metropolitan area: major railway routes

Chapter 1

恋

BE TOGETHER?
AUSTRALIA
HERE WE COME

There are not many things people really want to do in a lifetime. In my case, only three. I never want to be stuck in the same place; I always want to pursue the best, reach for the pinnacles in life; and I want to love women.

JJ and I. Our love has crossed countless contemporary social boundaries; we're lesbians, have a seventeen-year age gap and different nationalities. So, knowing that we couldn't be legally married, when JJ was forced to return to university in Australia in order to qualify for a Japanese working visa, I left Japan behind without hesitation. How can I describe that blue sky, that wide open land? My unexpected Australian experience appeared to fall from the clouds.

It was one Saturday when the first cold autumn winds had started to blow.

That night, I'd gone out to a small women-only club in Shinjuku Ni-chōme. The club was held in a cramped communal building in a narrow lane lined with steel and wooden constructions piled one atop another. I walked slowly up the tiny staircase and opened the door I knew so well. Through the pounding music I sensed that "today" was different, although I wasn't exactly sure why.

I glanced through the darkness to confirm my instincts. Sitting at the centre table was a long-haired woman. It had to be her first time to Ni-chōme. Women in designer suits, some with crew cuts, some with long bobbed hair, were milling around changing seats, cutting in and out and generally vying for her attention. It was a bit like a television dating show.

"I'm not interested, sorry." One down. Two down. No luck there! I soon found myself looking on and laughing along with Ms Straight-long-hair. The instant she caught sight of me she turned and asked, "Can you speak English?"

"Only a little. Why?"

"That blonde sitting over there, she's *gaijin* isn't she? I'm dying to speak to a *gaijin*. Will you translate for me, please?"

Eh! What? A *gaisen*? You mean, she's only interested in foreigners? I didn't come out with the intention of *gaijin* cruising with a *gaijin* specialist. "You know, I think it's rude to go up and talk to someone just because they're *gaijin*."

"You think so? But don't you even want to talk, just a little bit?" I looked in the direction she was pointing. Standing conspicuously way over at the corner of a far table was Ms Platinum-blonde-long-hair-blue-eyes.

Lesbian gatherings have always had an international flavour due to the strong information exchange network developed to counteract the terrible isolation that contemporary society enforces. Talking to foreigners at places like this has never been a big deal. That in itself is great, but there is one aspect which concerns me: the relentless inundation of English.

Whenever people, particularly the Japanese, go overseas (be it to Asia or Africa or wherever) we are convinced we must speak English. Native English speakers, what's more, consider it a matter of course to speak English in whichever country they visit. English inundates you wherever you travel worldwide. It is a problem linked not only to language; it also goes deeper to the relations between country and country, race and race, people and people.

"No, I don't really," I replied bluntly in answer to Ms Straight-long-hair's earlier question. That Japanese want to speak in English to white Anglo-Saxon *gaijin*, not in the languages of Asia or Africa to people from those regions, is part of our *gaijin* complex. It testifies to the depth and strength of our prejudicial tendencies. I promised myself there was no way that I was going to speak to that *gaijin*.

Usually I would have been able to forget Ms Platinum-blonde-long-hair-blue-eyes. But for some reason when I looked over at her again I was overcome by an unbearably strange sense of longing.

Hmph! Why should I speak to her? Oh, but I want to. Ohhh, the party's nearly over. I finally approached the *gaijin* woman who had got me so wound up.

"Will you speak Japanese?" I asked in English.

"*Hai, hanasemasu, yo.*" She replied in fluent Japanese.

"Gee, your Japanese is very good." I was convinced she wouldn't be able to understand anything difficult so I started the conversation off simply. Yet what came back was perfect Japanese. She said she was Australian and had been in Japan a couple of months. Her name was JJ.

"You really can speak Japanese."

"Of course. This is Japan, it's usual to speak Japanese."

"Oh, of course. Natural as crackers!"

JJ laughed at my old joke. "So many Japanese people come up and talk to me just because they want to try out their English. Because I'm a *gaijin*. But you asked straight up 'can you speak Japanese?' You're the first person who's ever done that."

I went bright red.

"So many people seem to want to learn English for no specific reason. They all ask the same things. Even tonight. 'Are you seeing anyone?' 'What's your type?' Always the same questions. At last, I've finally met someone who can hold an interesting conversation." Well, well. Perhaps it was coincidence, but JJ and I were talking openly about ourselves within minutes of meeting each other.

I live in a one-room apartment in outer Tokyo with my fifteen-year-old cat Nyan Nyan. I work freelance because I've always wanted to live as freely as possible without being tied to anything. Around this time I'd finished working with a theatre company I'd been involved with for some eight years and started with the production staff of a new group. JJ's eyes lit up when I told her I was busy selecting music for the next production. She said she'd been involved in theatre since she was seven. She'd performed in Japan, Canada and America as part of a youth theatre group. One of the Japanese production staff was even a mutual acquaintance.

Our conversation grew more intense, and before we realised it the party had finished. While the staff cleared up around us, JJ and I talked on until it was time for the last train. We walked together to Shinjuku station and bought our tickets. Hardly able to stop talking, we finally said goodbye after making arrangements to meet the next day.

The next day JJ and I went to a lesbian video showing. Over coffee afterwards we discussed the movies we'd just seen, then talked about the work of playwright Carol Churchill and the amazing spawning of Australian coral. We parted in time to catch the last train.

A week later a huge typhoon struck Japan.

"Even if it pours with rain, even if high winds blow, even if Godzilla swims in from Tokyo Bay and Mothra nests on Tokyo Tower, whatever happens, be there!" True to our telephone conversation promise, we met in the midst of torrential rain and laughed and joked around until the last train. A few days later, after going to the opening of a friend's exhibition, JJ and I had a quiet conversation. We only just made the last train. Time after time we separated at the last train, until one day JJ and I forgot all about that train.

Our romance had begun. I have no explanation. We both felt a desire to be with each other. There are so many chances in everyday places, like at school or work, for straight people to find "true love". But for us "homosexuals" it is relatively more difficult in this heterosexist society to find *the one* we feel we really need. You're not guaranteed to develop a deep attachment to the latest one-night stand from the lesbian scene, after all. Yet, even in this social environment, I have consistently fallen for women I've met in my everyday life surrounded by heterosexuals, at school or at work, some of them women who have "never been with a woman before". A simple love affair is a treasured thing. Extra-special relationships happen only a few a lifetime.

Within a few months of meeting each other in that Shinjuku "pick-up joint" our feelings developed into something deeper. There is a saying that love occurs three times in a life, and I began to believe it was true. Being with JJ washed away the combined happiness and trials of my numerous other relationships. The differences in our ages and countries of birth made no impact. To love and to be loved, a wonderfully rare occurrence—at once both precious and difficult.

When I met JJ she was on a working-holiday visa. She didn't explain her many reasons for quitting university and coming to Japan, just that she felt there was no point continuing to be in Australia. Apparently she felt her ability to speak Japanese provided only limited opportunities. Most were tied up with the financial market, doing office duties for businessmen who thought of nothing but exchange rates, or in the travel industry giving tours for Japanese tourists or working the front desk in hotel lobbies.

JJ quit university. Left home. Came out to family and friends. She said she felt she needed time to realign herself with the social expectations she felt closing in around her. She thought it better to separate herself from what she described as her own instability. She felt that in Japan, where she had spent a year at high school, that among the fascinating mix of traditional and contemporary beauty, here in the thriving polluted excitement of Tokyo, a place which shone in her eyes, she would surely find something.

The working-holiday visa system, which enabled JJ to stay temporarily in the country, differs in age restrictions from one country to another. It aims to enable students and young people to work while they spend an extended holiday overseas. The maximum time for Australians in Japan is one and a half years. Eight months after we met, JJ's time allowance had nearly reached its end. In order for her to remain in Japan, JJ had to get a working visa.

Until recently changing from a working-holiday visa to a working visa sponsored by a Japanese corporation or small business was relatively simple. During the last few years, however, the mass media had paid increased attention to the rising numbers of "illegal foreign workers" residing in Japan. The government pursuing this problem has monthly—almost daily—

tightened requirements, making it increasingly difficult for foreigners to work in Japan. The selection process is on a case-by-case basis and a multitude of provisions are attached to entry requirements. Currently, these provisions change constantly, so even a Japanese-speaking national like me has trouble understanding exactly what one needs to enter and work in the country. There was one stipulation which made JJ's chances of securing a working visa almost impossible. The government guidelines stated:

> Specialists in Humanities/International Services …
> 2 In cases where the applicant is to engage in a job requiring specific ways of thought or sensitivity based on experience with foreign culture, the following conditions are to be fulfilled. …
>   b The applicant must have three years experience in the relevant job, except in cases where the applicant has graduated from college and is planning to engage in translation or instruction in languages.

In other words, to obtain a working visa one must either be a university graduate, or have three years of career experience. Three years ago JJ was still a student. There is no way she could have amassed the necessary years of experience.

Without a visa there was no alternative but for JJ to return to Australia.

"What are we going to do? I won't go back to Australia on my own without you. It's boring, there's nothing for me to do, all anyone ever talks about is sports! What about the bogans who used to push me off my bike on the way home from high school? I don't care where it is, there's no way I want to go *anywhere* without you!" JJ gabbled in a panic.

I felt just the same. Maybe there was a way. JJ applied. Her application was knocked back. The next few weeks I spent every spare minute I had at the immigration department. On the fifth visit we discovered the officials had ever so politely added a new requirement. There was no way for there to be a way. The graduation certificate must be "the original", the actual diploma the dean hands over at the graduation ceremony. Bad luck for people like me who graduated over twenty years ago and have completely forgotten where they put their diploma. JJ found out from the embassy that this new requirement was a reaction against the fake certificates available in Thailand. Apparently they cost about $300.

A fake diploma sounded almost tempting. Years ago I had a friend who habitually shoplifted one item of food, an onion or something, from the upmarket supermarket Kinokuniya to share with her friends. I admired her immensely and could imagine a foreigner with a defiant look in their eyes confidently presenting a fake diploma to the immigration officials. Frankly, though, JJ and I were petrified of what would happen if the fake certificate was discovered as fake.

If we were a hot new straight couple, the story would end with one big cry of "Congratulations!" What? A wedding? But we were a hot new lesbian couple and, unless in Denmark, unable to have a wedding officially recognised. If I was male. If I was a man. (I might be friends with JJ, but never a lover.) With one marriage certificate, one piece of paper, JJ could get a three-year visa. Another case of blatant *discrimination*. And I promised myself I wouldn't use that word. The truth is, legal rights for same-sex partners are not recognised in Japan.

"Why! Why do we have to be flung apart?" For the first time in my life I tasted absurd panic. JJ's visa was to expire in a few months.

"What on earth are we going to do?" We investigated culture visas and student visas. A culture visa would give JJ another six months maximum. She could study any of the ancient arts recognised under this scheme, like *Nihon Buyō*, *shamisen*, *Noh* theatre or ceramic art. JJ didn't dislike ancient art; she had taken *Nihon Buyō* lessons while in Japan as an exchange student. She'd even performed *Sakura Sakura* in traditional costume. But JJ wanted to continue working in her current job, she didn't want to dance. Anyway, how long could she make a living by dancing *Sakura Sakura* and *Kurodabushi*?

"What about a student visa?" I started gathering information about academia. For foreign undergraduate students it wasn't easy to transfer credit points mid-course. For graduate students, transferring wasn't as difficult. From what I could gather, it was usual to enrol as a first-year student, and a certificate of first-level proficiency in Japanese was required. Some universities were willing to give credit for units taken in Australia. If it all went well, the minimum time would be two years. Graduation would take longer.

Some people went so far as to casually suggest, "It's only a piece of paper and everyone does it. Why not just get a paper marriage?" Marriage in Japan entails the married partners registering their names on the same family register (*koseki*). The woman usually transfers from her father's register to her husband's. How could JJ possibly justify registering her personage under the name of a man she hardly knew, just for the sake of a piece of paper?

"There's no way I'd do that."

"Me neither. I'm totally against it."

When the thing that "homosexuals" are fighting for most in this world is social recognition of their human rights, why on earth should a lesbian, who is being discriminated against on that very level, become part of the system that practises discrimination?

Adopting JJ was also an option. Apparently quite a number of lesbians in Japan have taken this course. I couldn't imagine us as "mother and child".

"JJ, I love you."

"I love you too, Mum." I did think we'd better avoid that one. We had already managed to skip over so many other social barriers. JJ appeared both confused and troubled by the question of adoption. She worried about the inevitable problems this would cause with my family, and was also uncomfortable with the constrictions lurking behind the concept of a pseudo mother-and-child relationship.

Everyone has their own fantasies about love and relationships. In accordance with those, some lesbians may equate adoption with marriage. My dream is different. In his discussion of same-sex male love in *Renai ron*,[1] Hashimoto Osamu writes that dreams of love are as common as driftwood on a beach. His lovers throw away conventions and promises of love, to fly beyond the earth. If these lovers fall to earth, it will be because of the gravitational pull of single pieces of paper. Unaware as we may be, all who live on earth are pulled down, along with all other matter, by one gram of gravity. People who have rocketed beyond the stratosphere say they truly appreciate the weight of that load.

We love each other enough to marry, but we won't. Not to have the gravitational pull of one piece of paper is far more wonderful. JJ and I thought. What way is there of of staying together without being bound by a piece of paper? It was a desperate situation. Just like love upon the chopping board.

---

[1] *Theories of love*, Tokyo: Kodansha, 1986.

JJ and I composed ourselves and thought again.

"The most important thing is for you to get a working visa so you can work without restrictions. What's the quickest way of graduating that will let you do that? What about re-enrolling at uni in Australia?"

"It would only take a year."

"Really. Well, I'll go with you." It was almost frightening, the speed with which it was decided.

When I told my friends they were supportive. "Go. Go. You don't have to return if you don't want to. But remember, if you do break up, you can always come straight back. If you run out of money, let me know."

I didn't imagine JJ and I would separate on bad terms. I was more concerned about whether my cat Nyan Nyan would remain healthy and live until I got back from Australia. There were money issues, of course, work and similar problems, but Nyan Nyan was the only thing that really worried me. I also loved my Tokyo lifestyle in my small one-room apartment. The café near the park. Bookstores jammed with books. Long, stimulating conversations with quirky friends. The thrill and excitement of theatre production. Being backstage. Wild rehearsal sessions with Kinbiren, the band in which I'd been a sax player for nine years. Making a decision, however, is the major obstacle. Once something's decided, it's one mountain climbed, another mountain climbed, yet another. The engine starts to run.

"Will you really come with me? I feel terrible you have to do something so drastic for my sake. I'm so sorry that I'm Australian, not Japanese." JJ sighed with regret.

"It's not for your sake. I'm going for my own sake. I've lived independently so far for this very reason, so that in whatever circumstance I could be honest to myself and treat my sexuality as truly important. I'm out with all of my friends and I work freelance anyway. 'Living' doesn't mean staying tied to one place and one job. This is a great chance. I'll really be able to experience the Australian lesbian community if I'm there a year."

JJ's re-enrolment was soon organised. I apologised to the theatre staff for seeming irresponsible. "It's you, after all, Marou. There's no way we could stop you. Anyway, you'll probably get bored within a month. If you do, be sure and come right back," they said in mock encouragement.

I found a friend who would look after Nyan Nyan, searched for work I could do in Australia and ran around organising financial support. Meeting JJ made me determined once again to push as hard as I could against society's useless borders.

More than fifteen years ago the physics world proposed a new theory, the chaos theory, to explain the flow of weather and gushing water. This theory maintains that to the extent a butterfly beats its wings in Peking, the weather in New York will change; there is no telling what effect even the smallest events may have. There is no way of telling exactly what people may do, or how they might mess up.

My going to Australia was a case of "See, I thought so." Really very strange.

Chapter 2

Love **WHY JAPAN?**

As usual, I was slightly disoriented as I made my way to the Immigration Department. I hadn't relied on maps in Perth. In Tokyo it was rare to successfully find a place with only the address as a guide. At the model agency where I worked I often took models to auditions, and these experiences had made me slightly more map-literate. I was no longer gripped by absolute panic when I emerged from the underground to surroundings nothing like the piece of paper in my hand. My record time for being lost was one and half hours. I'd spent that time searching for a job interview near Ginza. After five phone calls asking for clearer directions, they'd interviewed me out of pity, I'm sure. I didn't get the job, but I hadn't outdone that time record in the year since. Now I had only walked about five hundred metres before I realised I was going completely the wrong way.

A concreted river ran to the left. I checked my position on the mud map and turned to walk alongside it. Paths lined both sides of the fence. Huge grey slabs led down to a brownish-green trickle. The water itself was a familiar colour, but the narrow road running alongside was a little wider than in other areas of Tokyo. Interspersed trees broke the lines of houses. They created a sense of space despite a seemingly endless row of washing threaded through poles on second-storey verandahs. There was nothing special about this suburb of the metropolis.

Once in the Immigration building I took the required number. I sat on one of the plastic seats by the entrance and checked the documents in my envelope. Records of the model agency's financial status, charter copies, bank statements, letters of recommendations from the director of staff and company sponsor. My CV was a little on the short side, but as a "university dropout" I hadn't done too badly. I slipped my hand on the paper below. These pledges of sponsorship and guarantees of a healthy monthly salary would surely support my application to change to a working visa. I didn't anticipate any problems.

The woman behind the counter called my number. I smiled as I put my application into her hands. She looked a little annoyed at the inconvenience of an envelope. Apologising, I placed the documents on the counter one by one. Her eyes were already skimming through my application form. Before I had time to feel anxious she looked up at me.

"Sorry, we can't accept your application."

My stomach flipped. I tried to remain calm.

"Um. Are there some documents missing? If you'd like I can ring the office."

"You haven't graduated from university. See here," she pointed to the guidelines. "For this visa you must have a certificate of graduation."

My palms poured sweat. Tears stung my eyes. I could feel my chin sag and my lips quivered big time. I felt a tear slide over my eyelashes and tried to hold back more.

"The requirements are very clear. No university degree, no graduation certificate, no hope of applying. Here is an application for a six-month extension on your working-holiday visa. Fill that out and bring it back to me. Remember, this is the final extension you'll be permitted."

I saw a fleeting smile of compassion before she reached over to call the next number. My application had been rejected before it had even been made. In the middle of the blue lino Immigration floor I attempted to hide my sobs. From the non-chalant looks I figured hysterical foreigners weren't uncommon.

Four years ago I had been greeted at Narita airport by a group of middle-aged men. The January air was colder than anything I'd imagined. Winter underwear bought in Perth was no match for the easterly winds blown over the sea from Siberia. On the bus ride from the airport to my new home I became painfully aware that I was suffering not merely from temperature shock, but from a major communication problem. Two months of night-school Japanese had only prepared me for mundane greetings. Here I was faced with men, six of whom were going to be my host fathers. All I could do was fumble hello and try to pronounce my name in unfamiliar syllables. If I thought hard I could roll off the days of the week and the months of the year, but that didn't seem an appropriate first impression builder. In a series of briefings on Japanese culture leading up to my departure, I'd learnt what shape the toilets were, how to have a bath and how important taking off my shoes was going to be. Nothing had prepared me for the adrenalin rush of introducing myself on a handheld microphone over bumpy Chiba roads. In close to two hours we made it to Saitama prefecture and "home". I made the journey without embarrassing myself too much. I lugged my heavy blue suitcase up to my room on the second floor. I was surprisingly calm unpacking my clothes.

Suddenly I had a sister ten years younger and an obnoxious brother a year below her.

"*Isu!*" My host brother charged into my bedroom screaming. "Chair!" I yelled back through my teeth. His favourite game was coming into my room, pointing to objects and shouting out their names, before jumping into my closet and singing loudly to my clothes. For a while we had an arrangement. I exchanged one English word for one Japanese. The novelty wore off when I gained enough language to tell him he wasn't welcome to sing at my skirts any more.

My first host family eased me into school life. On my first visit to high school I was surprised to discover the complex stood in the middle of rice fields. Two large buildings housed the classrooms and offices. Racks of shoes filled the expansive communal entrance hall. Each student was allocated a shoe box where they placed their indoor school shoes overnight. There was commotion every morning as stragglers who arrived just before roll call hurried to change shoes. I hadn't yet purchased the indoor shoes and couldn't wear my outside ones beyond the shoe boxes. The headmaster indicated slippers my host parents and I were expected to wear. Thongs were banned for safety reasons at high school in Perth. I thought it strange here that slippers were presented to visitors. I was too large to fit into any of the ready-made uniforms and it was a few weeks before one my size could be made.

"Please, take good care of me," I stumbled over the formulaic greeting. With frozen slippered toes I stood out in my exchange student uniform on my first day as a second-year senior high school student.

The principal showed my host mother, father and I through the entrance of the school, and a buzz followed. We walked up one set of stairs to the staff room. The teachers' desks were lined face to face in rows. A huge whiteboard stood at the front of the room.

"*Shitsurei shimasu*," a student entering knocked on the door, excused herself with a bow and then walked in. Everyone seemed to be saying the same thing. A teacher with a chunky jaw got up from his desk and strode over.

"Welcome to our school," he smiled. This stranger was to be my homeroom teacher.

In a brief flash my host parents had abandoned me. They were whisked back to the principal's office for green tea and a chat. My homeroom teacher smiled again, "Come on. I'll show you around." I was relieved when it finally sunk in that I could understand him. He taught English and for the first two months of school was my link to communicative competence. He led me down some stairs and through a roofed passageway cutting across the gravelled outer yard. Corridors running overhead linked the two blocks of the four-storey complex. Bicycles were parked in rows on either side on the ground-floor walkway. Kids stuck their heads out of windows and pointed. "There. That's her. The foreigner." Without knowledge of Japanese it was impossible to tell if they were cheering or jeering. I put on the friendliest face I could conjure.

My homeroom was at the end of another long, foot-scuffed corridor on the first floor. More than forty desks crammed into five perfect lines. One desk stood vacant near the teacher's dais. From the next day my body would spill out of it and into the space of the boy next door.

"This is our new student from Australia. She'll be joining our class from tomorrow." I could barely understand my own name as the teacher spoke it.

A row of winter coats covered the back wall. We were warmed by a huge old boiler positioned at the front of the class.

I'd heard about central heating in colder climates, maybe it was a North American thing? My mind wandered. Standing in this classroom in a school surrounded by rice fields, my preconceived ideas of Japan as a super techno culture disappeared. There were no computers, no high-tech video screens, students didn't appear to be plugged into their desks. My wooden desk had a space underneath for my books, a hook on the side for my lunch bag. My pre-arrival promise on the plane from Perth not to compare or critique this new culture was the best decision I made. The worst? The sanitary goods with which I'd lined the bottom of my suitcase. The warnings of difficulties buying tampons for unmarried women proved to be nothing more than propaganda. I was soon the proud owner of a cute drawstring bag for all my menstrual paraphernalia.

Every day I bee-lined to the staff room. The homeroom teacher and I had a pact. While he was teaching I borrowed his desk and worked to learn one or two lines of the alphabet. Copying from the list he'd given me, first I'd write the characters in lines down the page. Cover them. Try to write them from memory; check and recheck. Inevitably they were facing the wrong way, had bits added or parts missing. He would test me in the ten-minute break between classes. After weeks of this pattern I finally learnt two sets of forty-six characters. By spring I was following simple conversations. In March, when I moved to my second host family, I began to keep a diary.

My mind flicked over these memories as I tried to gain the composure to make a phone call to Marou. In Saitama prefecture four years ago I'd developed a deep and colourful confidence. I was a total unknown and had the freedom to make myself into whatever I wanted. It was an experiment in self. Okay, whenever I bought a pair of knickers at the local supermarket the whole school knew the next day, but at least no one commented on the cigarettes I bought in vending machines at least one kilometre from the town centre. I was a novelty. Not just to those around, but to myself. My entire world crashed when I turned my back on Saitama and boarded the plane to Perth. Nothing prepared me for the reverse culture shock there, my own feelings of incompetence. I felt intense loneliness for the person I had become, and gradually became lost in the sea of my unknown desires. Compared to the freedom I discovered in country town Japan, the air in Perth was solitary confinement.

"They refused your application?" Marou's voice felt calm as it slid through my ears. There was no anger, that was yet to come.

Walking back from the Immigration Office my mind fell to the ground. I kicked my thoughts and wondered at my perpetual stupidity. Eight months ago in a tiny Ni-chōme bar I had met a woman who'd actually given me love. Visa-less and in love, I snorted. How on earth was I going to get over this obstacle? I looked up to the sky. Not even a speck of blue to console me. Never again would I let myself believe in anything before it happened. Glumly, I purchased my ticket and got on the train. In all my joints I felt sure this was going to be the beginning of another decision-making journey.

Chapter 3

恋 **GAYS AND JUNKIES AND PROSTITUTES**

JJ left Tokyo one step ahead of me.

I watched the sun set into the far side of the runway at Kuala Lumpur, the stopover point on this my solo journey, and mused over my hectic Tokyo life.

Anything is possible.

My thoughts turned to Nyan Nyan, my dear old cat left in the care of a friend, and mixed feelings churned inside. Despite my concerns for leaving her, I couldn't bring Nyan Nyan with me. A vast array of the earth's rare animals inhabit Australia, so getting a cat through immigration is extremely difficult. The effect of imported European animals has already been felt on the native ecosystem, and abandoned pets are a serious social problem.

I raised Nyan Nyan to have the freedom to be where she liked when she liked. I'm sure being locked up in a plane for a long flight, then quarantined in an unfamiliar place would definitely shorten her life span. What might be only slightly stressful for humans would surely be the death of a cat. After fifteen years together, numerous changes of address, budget-breaking re-wallpapering and replastering, all without any real trouble from rental property owners, I've ensured Nyan Nyan developed affection for humans. If the worst happened and her owner died, she would be well looked after by my friends. I couldn't kill her by putting her through all that confinement. I'd never be able to explain it to the cat sitters.

Anxiety sank to the bottom of my heart as the sun set over Kuala Lumpur.

I arrived in Perth, Western Australia, at one hour past midnight.

JJ and her childhood friend Kelly were waiting with worried looks. Considerable time had passed since the plane had landed and there'd been no sight of me. JJ was panicking that I'd been refused immigration for some reason. "Suspicious behaviour", "drugs" or "insufficient monetary funds for the proposed length of stay" were conceivable reasons. I could have easily been stopped for any of these, especially as I was carrying a year's supply of medication in my suitcase. You see, I'm asthmatic, prone to catching cold, and I also suffer from allergies. JJ had thought of all possibilities and two days before leaving Tokyo had typed an explanatory note for me to carry.

We'd only been separated for a day and a half, yet it seemed we hadn't seen each other in years. JJ called out and, unconcerned for the crowd of people she pushed through, ran towards me with hugs and kisses.

It is impossible to survive in Perth without a car, and Kelly had been kind enough to drive out for my midnight arrival in her purple Ford, which I later named "Sexual Violet". When JJ came out to Kelly, her response had been "Yeah …". It had made no difference to their friendship whatsoever. My sexuality is no issue to my friends either. Exactly eighteen hours earlier in the first light of a cold February morning, two of them had seen me off at Narita airport. Thinking I might not be able to eat steamed rice for a while and knowing how much I loved it, they'd even brought along *onigiri*.

"Hey, were you gals always this nice?!" Their thoughtfulness stung tears in my eyes.

Stepping out of Perth airport was like walking into the tropics. It was the middle of summer and the night was hotter than an average Tokyo summer day. The three of us headed to another friend's house. We were going to stay with Nikki until we got settled.

Nikki lived alone in a three-bedroom house with a big back yard in the northern suburbs. She had set up a double futon for us and kindly said, "You can stay here until you find your own place." JJ's mum had also been delighted to hear that JJ was planning to return to study and would be in Perth for a prolonged period. Knowing of our relationship she had offered, "JJ, your room is still empty and we have another one spare, for a start you could live here for a while." JJ had only managed to reply vaguely to that proposal.

"Live with the family? I'm really touched that she offered, but we'd have to sleep in separate rooms, in separate beds. Any of us kids would."

"Mmmm."

"From her point of view she probably wants to think we don't have sex. I mean, I can understand how she feels but there's no way I'm going to sleep apart from you." Until university started, JJ and I happily stayed with Nikki.

Standing on Nikki's front lawn I was enthralled by the sense of space. Australian suburban housing is incomparable to Tokyo. Our one-room apartment has bedroom, study, kitchen and storage space squeezed into eight metres by ten metres. It doubles as both laundry and washing line on washing days. Here, over the back of Nikki's orange roofing, was a wide expanse of green, green grass.

From across Nikki's fence I could hear: "Splash! Zaboom! Yeoiww! Splash!"

"Uh-huh, next door has a pool." I suppose in a city where the temperature goes above forty degrees it had to be expected. Living here I gradually came to understand the middle-class Australian dream. First you start with a home in the outer suburbs. Then upgrade the model of your car, get a second one, buy a caravan, purchase a small boat, put a pool in the backyard, invest in a holiday home. I'm not exactly sure where it finishes. It probably extends endlessly to a small yacht, light aircraft, art objects, private beaches overseas, personal islands. In Tokyo it's common for a mortgage to be passed from one generation to the next; even a mortgage on a small apartment may take over fifty years to repay. With unemployment levels so high in Perth, especially youth unemployment, it was surprising to see what seemed like such a rich and abundant housing market.

"I'm thinking of getting a tent, so maybe we could go out camping some time." Perhaps Nikki was currently part of the "Australian dream" school.

JJ is part of what you might call the "move away from Australia" school.

"You know, I really hate suburbia," she said to me as I gaped open-mouthed at the snaking row of lawns. "I don't want to be stuck in the same place I was born, doing the gardening and paying off a mortgage for thirty years. Each to their own, but one year is quite enough for me." She repeated this again and again as if to remind us both of our short-term plans.

Only one other thing irked JJ as much as the thought of being stuck in Perth indefinitely—the general consensus to use Japanese purely as a money-making tool. The Japanese language department to which she returned was situated in the economics faculty and, regardless of her personal desires, JJ's university lecturers seemed keen she use her Japanese to engage in government work or become involved in the international economic market upon graduation. JJ had a different kind of "dream". The phrase "for life" would never come out of her mouth, not in a discussion on her present or her future.

"No matter how well you understand that you will continue to change, the future will always outstrip anything you can imagine," she believed.

JJ and I had come to Perth with the expressed purpose of JJ finishing university so that we wouldn't be forced apart again. Even so, we couldn't take advantage of Nikki's kindness forever. Before uni started and things got busy, we had to find a house.

"So, where are we going to live?" When the subject of finding a location came up, not only myself, who had been on holidays but never lived overseas, but even JJ, who was supposed to hate this town, started to get excited. JJ and I, who loathe waking up before midday, suddenly found ourselves up early each morning strolling to the deli near Nikki's to buy the morning paper. We wanted to get in quick on the for-rent and motoring pages.

Just when I'd managed to remember where the bus stop was, how to read the timetable, how to pay the fare, where to get off and how to make a phone call if I got lost, we bought a 1976 Colt Galant. We jumped into our dream car, Ginga (Galaxy), and set off to look at the properties from the paper that we'd marked with an asterisk. Apartments with joint pool facilities, flats less than thirty seconds walk from a tropical blue sea, old-style houses with antique floor boards. My mind wandered from one place to the next, unable to make a decision from the range of housing, all at cheap rents impossible to find in Tokyo. JJ, on the other hand, seemed to have decided in which area of Perth she wanted to spend a year with me.

"So, where do you want to live?"

"Northbridge."

"Why?"

"You know, people reckon that it's 'dangerous' because it's filled with 'gays' and 'junkies' and 'prostitutes'. But I've never once thought of Northbridge as dangerous. There are so many cute old houses still standing, and heaps of cafés and clubs nearby. In fact it's quite fashionable to live there now." I'm always a sucker for the "fashionable", so we set out right away to investigate Northbridge.

The tables spread out on the sidewalk of the Italian café we passed were covered with bright table cloths. JJ pointed out the club Connections and the pub where the lesbian and gay community congregated for the Sunday session. There was a bookstore which stocked lesbian and gay books, the latest releases, and magazines. In the space of a few blocks there was every imaginable type of restaurant: Chinese, Indian, Lebanese, Thai, Vietnamese, Japanese. In ten minutes I could amble to the art gallery and library, and only a little further into the heart of Perth city centre. In a city spread so far along the coast it was dreamlike to find a place from where I could walk to anywhere I wanted to go.

There was no hint of anything "dangerous": in fact, I felt a sense of relief every time I walked past another gay person. In a world where heterosexual culture is so strictly enforced, when we are verbally harassed and physically abused just for walking along the street, it's unusual to find a place where lesbians and gays can walk relatively free of tension. In Japan few people realise JJ and I are a couple. When we travel on the subway, JJ, being a blonde blue-eyed *gaijin*, is often leered at by Japanese men. It's quite disgusting. Men who sidle up to stare at her breasts and legs are perhaps on the "lighter" end of the scale than those men who shout "hello" across train platforms, or who follow us off the train, eavesdrop on our conversations or even throw their own comments into our personal exchanges. I felt pure happiness strolling past lesbians and gay men on a public footpath in Northbridge. Although I'd had my heart set on living close to the beach, I soon understood JJ's strong desire to live here.

"Okay. Northbridge it is."

We stumbled across a two-bedroom semi-detached house with a small garden in Northbridge for the reasonable price of $125 a week, just before JJ's university semester was due to commence. It was an old building with high ceilings which faced onto a narrow road. The living room was almost twice the size of our Tokyo apartment, the rent almost half, and we would even have our own laundry. The kitchen was decorated in bright orange Italian tiles, the bathroom in blue. I could imagine the kitchen being used as an example of interior design in a showroom for expensive Tokyo residences. A barbecue set sat waiting in the back garden and there was even a small shed. We joked that we could have rented the shed to another couple had this been Tokyo. I couldn't help thinking that Nyan Nyan would have been overjoyed in this open space.

The property owner's mother lived in the house next door. She was a friendly woman who had emigrated from Italy over thirty years before. For some reason, I was just a little bit nervous. Fifteen years ago, when I visited a friend who had emigrated to Italy, I'd been overwhelmed by the level to which heterosexism was part and parcel of the Catholic religion and daily life. For the duration of my stay, total strangers were constantly asking me,

"So, are you married?" It was like an alternative form of greeting. Going out to a restaurant, to the theatre, being invited to a friend's house for dinner; all activities were based on the female–male couple unit. It seemed like some kind of offence for an adult female to act on her own. My sudden irrational anxiety at the thought of this kind-looking woman next door finding out about our relationship was vaguely understandable. But after coming this far there was no way I wanted to crawl back into the closet and camouflage my sexuality.

It was a Sunday, a few days after we'd moved. We invited some of JJ's old friends and some new acquaintances over for a house-warming party in our new abode. Kelly was the only straight woman. She giggled and commented, "Everyone's talking to me as if I was a lesbian, it's quite amazing. Usually in conversations everyone talks with the presumption you're straight, but it's the opposite here. This is really interesting." She seemed to be enjoying the reversal of events.

The sky was a wonderful deep blue. We took our chairs outside and chatted over beer and wine, enjoying the beautiful weather. I suddenly realised we were all talking in very loud voices about a lesbian party held the other week. One flimsy latticework fence separated our garden from next door. The property owners and their high-school-aged daughters were visiting their grandmother. Every now and again either one of the owners or their children came into the garden next door and glanced over at us, listening in to our conversation. I began to get concerned. I wondered whether it was going to be okay.

The following day JJ had an early lecture, and I decided to go to the university library to read. I got ready and walked out the front door. JJ accompanied me outside. The woman next door was watering her flowerbeds.

"Hi. It's a beautiful day isn't it."

"Yeah, it really is a lovely morning. Those flowers are pretty."

"These have a wonderful perfume. Smell them. See. Good huh," she said snapping a white flower from its stem and passing it over to JJ.

"Wow, these are good."

"Please, take one."

"Thanks. See you later."

"Bye, have a good day."

We climbed into Ginga and were sent off by the woman next door waving us goodbye. I felt oddly relieved.

"Homosexual, heterosexual, Japanese, *gaijin*—I've always been against lumping people together into over-generalised categories and ignoring the individual, yet here I've done exactly that myself." Driving into the university carpark I realised that, along with society at large, I too had to work on resisting over-generalisations and strive to develop greater sensitivity to complicated issues.

Some weeks later I woke at daybreak to the sound of strong wind and heavy rain. The end of summer in Perth comes with storms. Despite the fierce storm howling outside the window, JJ continued to sleep deeply.

"Ouch!" I kneaded the pressure points on the soles of my feet, tired from continuous dancing. Perth's population is only one-tenth of Tokyo's, yet there were so many people at a single Sunday session. A little freedom makes a huge difference, it seems. Pubs of that size don't exist in Tokyo. Ni-chōme pubs, which are mostly for gay men only, are merely small rooms with a name. They'd accommodate a hundred people at the very most. The first full-scale lesbian dance club in Tokyo, Mona Lisa, had started monthly before we left. At its most crowded about a hundred lesbians partied in the basement space. The clubs got so crowded at the weekends here in Perth, you had to queue to get in. Queuing at the club Connections I discovered that, although clubbing is fun, it can also take courage. It seems that violent homophobic neo-Nazi types who believe they have the right to kill are a worldwide phenomenon.

Until coming to Australia, the only "bashing" I'd ever heard of was "Japan bashing". I first saw the words "gay bashing" at the gay and lesbian association at JJ's university. JJ discovered the club on orientation day and got a copy of their homophobia action kit. I noticed the "Stop the Bashing" poster stuck on the door when we went to a meeting at the beginning of semester. At the time I was a little startled but didn't really comprehend. On the way home near Northbridge in Ginga JJ suddenly gasped, "Shit! I don't believe it."

"What? Don't scare me! What is it?"

"The graffiti on that wall over there while we were stopped at the lights. How sick!"

"What did it say?"

"Keep Australia beautiful. Bash a gay a day."

"How disgusting!"

A little while after, a documentary about gay bashing was broadcast on TV. I was shocked at how frequent bashings are. The very fact that lesbian and gay documentaries are actually broadcast indicates the success of the gay and lesbian liberation movement in Australia. But oppression and liberation exist back to back in any era, lesbian bashing too. Heterosexism seems more entrenched in Western cultures than in Japan. When I was at high school, groups of girls and boys alike would talk with their arms around each other's shoulders. Good friends always walked hand in hand, in school and out. As Western heterosexism has

恋

penetrated further into Japanese society it's rarer to see friends holding hands in public, but there is still a lot of physical contact between same-sex friends at school. I could only laugh when, holding hands with JJ walking through Shibuya once, a white woman pushing a baby chair screamed, "Oh my god! Lesbians!"

One Saturday night we were queued outside Connections. JJ had just commented that it would be at least another ten minutes until we got in. Suddenly a group of men crossed over from the other side of the street and shouldered their way through our line. They pushed past JJ and I and deliberately knocked one of the young gay guys in front of us. "Move, ya poof!" they squawked and lumbered off flapping their arms.

It lasted all of ten seconds. Time seemed to have frozen still.

JJ squeezed my arm tight and in a small voice whispered, "You just have to ignore people like that." She looked as if nothing had happened, but her grip hurt my arm and she was shaking. If they come back and do even the smallest thing to JJ, I'll fight them to death. Anger boiled through my body. I clenched my teeth.

"And they say *we* can't walk straight!" One person's well-timed words loosened the tight air.

Philosophy of the absurd maintains that humour is born where there is no resolution. If we took up against every kind of harassment we would only repeat and repeat bloody violence. Buddhism believes that Maitreya, the bodhisattva, symbolically refused redemption and said, "Redeeming oneself alone is not enough. Only after five thousand, six hundred and seventy million years of saving all who follow can peace be found." If this is true, it will be a long, long time before people stop oppressing, dominating and violating others. This dream merits coming true by the twenty-first century, let alone in a stupefying five thousand, six hundred and seventy million years.

JJ heard from the campus club that bashings were more common in private schools than in public schools. JJ went to a public school and remembers a gay guy from the year above who was ostracised. A few years ago, the story of the principal of a prestigious Catholic school who included messages opposing the Sydney Gay and Lesbian Mardi Gras in his new year welcoming address was widely publicised. It makes me wonder how young gay and lesbians sent by their parents to schools like that survive.

Such stories take me back twenty-odd years to my high school days in rural Japan.

Twenty-something years ago I was still living in the country town where I was born. At that time in Japan, Van, Jun and McSister were the trendy fashion brands. My one big pleasure was coming home from school, ripping off my navy blue uniform, changing into a fresh, earthy-coloured Jun jumper, a dark blouse and pair of coloured jeans, taking a twenty-minute train ride to the nearby city and making my way down to the one and only big bookstore on the main street. I didn't even look at Terayama Shūji's best-selling psychedelically illustrated poetry books. One by one, like a good little high school student, I bought Dostoyevsky's *The Brothers Karamazov* and *The Possessed*. The paperback edition of *The Brothers Karamazov* comprised six volumes and, being about God, desire and other worldly things, was difficult to read. I read novels to escape the society around me.

One day I was called to the staff room and issued a warning.

"You. Where did you go after school yesterday!"

"Hmm, to the book shop."

"What were you doing there?"

"I bought a book."

"That's all?"

"Let's see, after that I went to the food section of the department store and bought some things for dinner like Mum had asked me to."

"I didn't ask that! You were wearing men's blue jeans, weren't you!" The only jeans this teacher could imagine were blue jeans.

"No, I was wearing brown women's jeans."

"Liar! Don't you think that what you've done is wrong!"

"Huh? What's wrong?"

"You! Don't answer back!"

"No, si-ir."

"Detention. After school." Having no idea whatsoever as to why I was being punished, I stayed behind after school until the teacher allowed me to go home.

The next week there was a morning assembly. The principal addressed the whole school in a heavy tone. "Last week a student from this school, a *girl*, was found roaming around the main street in men's blue jeans and a bright red jumper. It is inexcusable for a girl to wear men's clothes!"

Bad colour coordination, and they're not men's clothes. I couldn't believe it. It was a waste of time trying to explain the epitome of trendiness, Twiggy and unisex fashion to teachers whose fashion sense had ceased developing. I just kept quiet.

Late one night over coffee I recounted this story to JJ, Nikki, and our new friends Kathy and Trish. We were all tired from dancing at the club, but Kathy and Trish, who are around my age, perked up wide-eyed. "It was the same here twenty years ago. If you wore jeans you were always yelled at to put on a skirt!"

"I don't know even now why it warranted such a fuss."

"They say 'attack is the beginning of defence'. They must have had some issue they were burning to protect."

"When people get really angry and hysterical it's usually because they have some big identity problem that they're trying to protect."

I've no desire to seriously debate with religious types calling people the devil and educators who get hysterical about jeans. If anyone changes their view of me because I love women or happen to wear jeans, that is entirely their problem; it has nothing to do with me. I will make my own truth known; the rest is their concern. If they base their identity on pettiness, then it will be shaken by pettiness because what really shakes someone is their own person, their own self.

In Japan, minority-bashing has been around at least since my adolescence. Educators' words caused pain to me and thousands of other young lesbians and gays. Unfortunately, the situation has not seen a great deal of change. In fact, as lesbian and gay liberation progresses, bashing becomes a problem which can't be pushed aside. Recent television programmes trying to "spot the gay" at beats are eerily foretelling. That is why the sight of lesbians and gays defiantly holding hands and showing their love openly in the street, despite the bashings, is inspirational.

JJ took my hand as we waited at the lights in Ginga. Regardless of why we were here, we were determined to make the most of our year in Perth. We had brought all of our savings plus the sum which our friends had lent to us, and we were still racked with concern as to how we were going to make it through the year. We would make do somehow. We had tasted the worst fear of all, that of forcible separation; compared to that threat, all other problems seemed insignificant.

A rainbow formed as the sky cleared of rain. With her hand firmly holding mine, JJ sped off towards the largest rainbow I had ever seen.

Chapter 4

JJ's PARENTS ALSO WORRIED

I had met JJ's mother and father for the first time in March 1991 when the two of us were on a carefree holiday in Australia. At that point we were still under the illusion that it would be easy for JJ to change her visa. We were staying with JJ's friend Terri, a nurse. The living room lights were off and Terri, Nikki, JJ and I were watching *Twin Peaks*, the hit series of the time. JJ and I dared not breathe as we sat as we'd been ordered and watched the show we'd been warned not to miss.

The detective took a bite of his donut.

The phone rang.

JJ answered it.

"We're going to see my mum and dad next Sunday, is that okay?"

Twin Peaks faded from before me the moment JJ whispered in my ear.

"Ohhhh." Meeting JJ's parents.

Japanese TV commercials flashed before me. The type where a young guy in a suit carrying a bouquet of flowers waits at the front door.

"Mr … Mr Tanaka. May I … May I have Yukiko's haaaannnd … hand in marriage …!" When ads like that are aired, I feel I've had weddings, brides—the complete package of ancient family adoration—forced at me. What utter nonsense. Yet, as soon as JJ said the words "meet my parents", my mind filled with images of flowers and suits and ties. What will I wear? What should I say? My heart raced. I spent the next few days absentmindedly.

I'll never forget the 5th of March. That was the big day.

JJ's parents were sipping cappuccinos as they waited at Miss Maud's in Fremantle. Sitting together at a plastic table on the raised brick paving tucked in an outer corner of the café, they looked extremely anxious. A sigh of relief passed between them as we sat down in the chairs opposite. It was the first time they'd been face to face with JJ in nearly a year. They'd obviously wondered what kind of person JJ's "girlfriend" was. A nervous smile passed over each of their faces. JJ had left Perth in the midst of unsettled family misunderstandings and it was almost as if they were soaking in all the ways she had changed.

JJ's father was a robust-looking gentleman, her mother gentle-eyed. I'd tried not to dress too casually and my clothes seemed stiff in the inner curve of the plastic chair. Work, life in Tokyo, what I had studied at university, family, my country town. Do you smoke? Do you drink alcohol? What kind of books do you read? The topic changed quickly as questions about me piled one upon another.

"Today's paper mentioned that SDP leader Doi might resign, is she popular in Japan?"

"From a Japanese person's point of view what should Perth do to improve its tourism?"

"On the surface Japanese traditional arts appear extremely beautiful, but as a woman living in Japan what is it actually like?" And so on. JJ's parents really liked to "discuss". We carried on talking happily after coffee and into dinner at a nearby Italian restaurant. My memory of that day is of enjoyable chatter.

Although JJ's parents understand she's a lesbian, it's not as if they haven't had problems with it. On the other hand, they don't appear to openly reject it either. They didn't go out of their way to focus on the potential seriousness of meeting their daughter's girlfriend. Instead, as I saw it, they started little by little, with a sense of humour and a great deal of love and trust, to try to begin to understand things they didn't. I immediately became a fan of JJ's parents.

Now that we were living in Perth I was amazed at how well JJ's family got on. Almost every week the family, married sisters and their husbands included, got together to enjoy doing something as a family. More surprisingly, most Perth restaurants and cafés were filled with family groups. Two-year-olds in prams dribbled icecream in cafés, quite different to other major cities I'd visited where individuals got together for lively conversations and espresso coffees.

On 1 May, Mother's Day, all the relatives gathered for a picnic in Kings Park. On the way home we invited JJ's parents for coffee in Northbridge. Here I had the opportunity to ask all the questions which had been burning inside since that first meeting over a year ago.

"Tell me honestly, what did you think of me the first time we met?"

JJ's mother answered instantly as if she had been waiting for my question. "Firstly, you looked so young. When I heard your age later I was really surprised. You had on a lovely suit, and those sunglasses made an impression. Until we spoke I didn't know anything about you, so my first impressions are very superficial. You were much more relaxed than I expected."

Appearance doesn't matter as long as you are true to yourself. Nonetheless, how I'd appeared to JJ's parents had been a big issue for me. "And?"

JJ's mum continued. "Talking to you what impressed me the most was that you really listened and answered our questions seriously. It was plain to see that you thought JJ was special."

"Mmm, mmm," JJ's dad nodded a few times from the seat beside her. "I think there are only two kinds of parents. Parents who love their children deeply and those who don't. Just those two. When JJ first confided her sexuality to us, it was really hard. We felt like our feet weren't touching the ground. We talked and talked that night about how it must be much more difficult for the child to confide than for the parents to hear. We said to ourselves that even if we didn't really understand we would look out for JJ because she must have trusted us as parents to be able to tell us. When she talked to us she didn't have a girlfriend, and we talked about that a lot as a couple after she'd gone to Japan."

Could you hope for more ideal parents? I looked at JJ's parents almost in wonder. Then, "Oh really?" JJ butted in, surprised. I was taken back by her cool response.

A little of what JJ had told me about Perth before going to Japan ran across the back of my mind. When she came out her mother apparently said, "JJ, it's alright. I nursed you from a child. You're mistaken, you're not a lesbian." Her father said, "Okay, JJ. Just don't tell anyone. I don't want to turn on the TV and see you marching at Mardi Gras." There was a huge gap between her parents as JJ had described them when she came out, and the kind, gentle ones speaking to us now. A lot seemed to have changed and I still couldn't understand why JJ would want to keep her distance from these loving, eloquent people who sat in front of me.

"Yes, that's how it was. And if she had a particular partner then we, as parents, would naturally be anxious as to what sort of person they were. So, until we actually met you we worried and worried about all sorts of things. But all of those concerns have disappeared since then. It was fun talking to you, and the two of you look like such good friends."

"But in actual fact our relationship is more than just friends. If you don't mind, I'd appreciate it if you could tell me how you feel about that." In journalistic fashion I dived a bit deeper.

JJ's dad took a deep breath. Her mum drank her coffee in a single gulp.

"Hmm. I suppose I still can't really comprehend that. For example, I can't even imagine myself what I would think if I saw you hugging like a couple. It might be alright, it might stop being alright." As her father spoke I could feel, almost telepathically, a tension beginning in JJ. "I suppose we really don't understand. But all we can do as JJ's parents is to trust her. It's JJ after all and we just have to trust her."

"Yes. JJ will always be our beautiful little JJ."

In her mother's words "beautiful little JJ" lay over twenty years of devotion for the daughter they had so lovingly brought up. I mused over the words, "trust", "love", "beautiful little JJ". Coming from the very different culture and language of Japan, I have no idea what meaning and strength those words hold in an Australian household. When JJ's father said something like, "If we trust our daughter and do all that we can, God will take care of the rest", I felt as if I had glimpsed the unique complexity of the honne (private self) and tatemae (public self) of Christian culture.

It seems that for many Australian lesbians, coming out begins with your own family and develops from there. All of the lesbians

I met, including non-political, non-feminist lesbians, were out to their families. It continues to honestly amaze me to hear of families who treat their daughter and her lover the same as legally married members of the family.

"When did you come out to your family?" It's a question I'm often asked in Perth. I never know what to answer.

My mother died after a long illness. Every time I went to the country to see her she would say, "It's fine as long as you're happy." It was almost habitual. The words "even if you're a lesbian" appeared unspoken. The nuance was that it was better left unsaid. In very Japanese style, sexuality was purposefully not mentioned outright. In the midst of not speaking, not discussing, we developed a mutual understanding. With no prior knowledge of the Japanese feudalistic family, it is exceedingly difficult to explain this irritating relationship. Rather than talking together openly, this "better left unsaid" relationship develops between family members regardless of whether one wants it to or not.

My father was a perfect example of a father in the period of high economic growth when the Japanese government announced its "income doubling programme". He worked two or three times as much as other people, rarely took holidays, and performed his duties to his family by driving his beloved imported car himself on Sundays. He was also unbelievably autocratic at home. In my house, women were not permitted to bath before men. When prior bathing was necessary, I had to walk down the long corridor to my father in the drawing room and sit *seiza* on the cold wooden floor outside the room. Then open the *fusuma* fifteen centimetres with both hands and bow deeply. While bowing in the cold corridor the solemn words "Please excuse my rudeness in going before you" had to be uttered. Difficult to comprehend now, but this was serious. Opening the *fusuma* with a bang and going in saying, "Hey Dad, I'm gonna have a bath first, okay" has a totally different ring to it.

No matter how extensively democratic education penetrated the school system, no matter that boys learnt domestic
science and girls acquired carpentry skills, the feudal era never
left our house. My father would sit cross-legged in the drawing
room chatting with his visitors late into the night. My mother
and I would sit *seiza* in the corridor with our heads bowed low. It
was no different to the middle ages, the Edo period. In my
household my father was lord of land and castle to an extent
that would shock most 1990s Japanese teenagers. In the name
of "tradition" and "Japanese culture", "differences" between
superior/inferior and female/male, which are essentially nothing
more than deeply held prejudices, seeped irreversibly into
everyday life.

On occasions when I was forcibly made to wear a kimono,
my father would roll around in high spirits. "I'll buy you some
kimono as a reward for looking so charming" was his attempt at
flattering me. But I'm not one of Pavlov's dogs. I want rights and
freedom more than a kimono. Now that I am far removed from
the restrictions of family I can appreciate traditional Japanese
aesthetics intensified in art forms such as kimono design,
architecture and landscaping. Restrictions that are forced into
your daily life as extensions of compulsive traditions are simply
too oppressive.

In an archaically constructed family like mine, opening your
heart and talking together definitely does not produce happy
results. It would be equivalent to the subordinates taking over
the superiors—in other words, a riot. As soon as I said things like
"Why must I do such things, Father?" in the super-polite language wives and daughters must speak in archaic family units, he
sputtered, "Because you're a girl!!!!" Discuss sexuality, ha! From
high school onwards my life was like a continuous domestic
version of the feminist war. To my domestic strikes and protest

actions against this ludicrous women's education my father never acted violently; he just stubbornly refused to lend his ears.

To speak with just an inkling of dissension in a tedious feudal household which can't move flexibly in response to new ideas or situations means the end of relationships. Consequently, matters that should be discussed are silently understood through a paradox that recognises them as "better left unsaid". Coming out itself is a complex process. Coming out openly to one's family is linked intrinsically to whether a relationship of open discussion has been built up within the family. In my family there was never any hope of discussing anything. It was astonishing to experience such vastly different family relations in Australia.

It was clear that JJ's parents were restless in their confusion of wanting to understand JJ, but not quite being able to. They went out of their way to accept me as JJ's partner. On the way home from the café JJ's father said to me, "When I first met you I only thought of you as JJ's girlfriend, but now you are a special friend of ours. I might get it wrong sometimes, but I want to respect your father. After all, he brought up such a wonderful person as you."

I doubt if my father has ever anguished, the way JJ's parents have, over not being able to understand me. Formerly a commissioned officer in the imperial army, he still calls foreigners "hairy whites". The gap between us is so deep that I have never spoken one word about sexuality to him. If we could help it, we wouldn't even want to approach the subject of relating to society, let alone lifestyles. JJ, who knew all of this, looked at me anxiously.

The four of us, JJ, her parents and I, became closer after that talk in the café, and often chatted on the phone and went out for coffee. I gradually came to feel envious of the relationship between JJ and her parents. It enabled open conversation not imaginable in Japan. I even thought that JJ's criticisms might been her "over-imagination".

The more conscious you become of each other's situation, the less often intricate misunderstandings between people surface in words or actions. Yet sometimes misunderstanding may be so deeply rooted that, without malice on anyone's part, it can suddenly be born even in the cheerful face of another. JJ and I were getting on so well with JJ's parents that we forgot the pain we had experienced numerous times before. JJ seemed to gradually begin to form a new, different kind of distance in her relationship with her parents.

Chapter 5

Love SEEDS OF RECONCILIATION

Walking down Dōgenzaka in Shibuya nearly two years ago I clutched a letter from my father in my hand. The model agency where I worked had recently offered me an apartment closer to the office. Consequently I'd moved from my six-mat room in the "*gaijin* house" I shared with four others. Canadian, Australian, Chinese and Argentinean, we'd shared pitted saucepans, bad television reception and the occasional slice of bread. "You pay 65 000 yen a month for this?" Marou stared surprised at the buckled, rotting *tatami* in my corner room. Stepping over empty coffee mugs, poetry notebooks, paint tubes and a week's worth of dirty clothes, she declared, "I can't see how you find the floor to sleep in this room." With a steady income only recently established, and in debt to the parents of a friend, I surprised her more when I told of how I recycled my soups and sauces to get three meals for the price of one.

I hadn't collected much in three months at the house and easily carried my possessions on the train south to the seedy apartment block off the Dōgenzaka hill. The building was ten storeys high and unimaginatively brown. Metres away, love-hotels enticed sex-hungry couples to "rest" in rooms for as little as 5000 yen an evening. Functionally, the 1970s architecture of the apartment block was an improvement on the two-storey

Ĺove

"*gaijin* house" nestled in the corner of a gravel carpark. Although I could no longer judge the change of seasons by my housemate's reactions to the arrival of hot drinks in the corner vending machine, my total daily train travel was cut down from almost two hours to just under ten minutes. Including walking time, I could be at the office twenty minutes after I left home.

"JJ," the boss chuckled as I answered the telephone at fifteen minutes past ten, "aren't you glad we don't have a time card system". I was still frequently late for our mid-morning start.

My new one-room apartment was sparse. I had no furniture. My old blue suitcase held most of the clothes that wouldn't fit on the metal rack substituting for a wardrobe. Marou let me use some of her leftover gift coupons to buy the futon spread over one corner of the floor. In mid-winter the space was cold. Sleeping on the hard concrete floor was difficult enough, let alone the intermittent sound of stiletto heels tapping along the corridors into the early hours of morning.

"There go the girls next door again," Marou grumbled into our 4 a.m. futon. The majority of occupants in the apartment block apparently operated date clubs or phone-sex clubs.

Marou was with me this morning of the letter. After a night on the cold floor she was quite anxious to return to her own cosy room. "I really need to read this letter," I explained, ducking into a cheap café selling coffee at 180 yen a cup. Dad was in hospital recovering from heart failure. He was scheduled for another operation. I could hardly read his straggling handwriting, which blurred before my eyes. For over a year I maintained things so that we'd hardly had any contact. Yet, here was my father speaking honestly in a letter filled with obviously difficult beginnings.

A year and half earlier I'd invited my parents for dinner at the restaurant where I'd waitressed before deferring from university. "I'm gay, I've changed my name, and I'm moving back to Japan in a month." After sushi, and before the teriyaki chicken, I exposed the reason behind my dinner invitation. Six months after moving out of my family's home I knew I had to make further changes. Two years of struggling to write university papers in English, of obtaining last-minute deadlines to counteract unintelligible sentences, left me convinced that my mental state had undergone major alteration. Neither monolingual nor bilingual, all action was frozen. My seventeen-year-old English-language self had difficulty realigning with the nineteen-year-old one who'd found self-confidence speaking fractured Japanese. Beyond this linguistic confusion, I finally understood sweet desire. I could no longer pretend the magazine models posted on my inner mind were merely adolescent adoration for female beauty.

New foundations of Australia's drive into Asia were being fuelled by returned exchange students like me, but the obvious economic bias made my yearning for human cultural contact stronger. Like others, I planned to become rich and famous in Tokyo, but not through processes of industrial exchange. During my year as an exchange student I was surprised at the number of foreign nationals who achieved celebrity status because they were not Japanese. Some spoke Japanese fluently; others merely took advantage of their native English abilities and white-skin privilege. White European and North American models featured in a large number of glossy advertising campaigns in the booming bubble-economy.

I convinced a friend there was money to be made in Japan. Naively, I planned to use my Japanese skills to sell him as a model before establishing my own television career. We would use the money we made to embark on projects overseas. I borrowed money from his parents, booked a flight and packed.

I saw Tokyo as my city. I felt sure I could conquer my confusion. Nikki and Terri had helped me orientate my sexuality, Kelly had quietly supported my emotional ups and downs. My personal survival strategy caused me to push my family away.

I could only guess that my coming out hadn't been easy for either Mum or Dad. I never asked. Never continued the dialogue. I'd anticipated a negative silence and like so many other lesbians I was afraid of risking possible rejections. My sisters and brother registered their understanding, but I was unable to accept the support they seemed almost unsure of how to offer. We floundered towards each other, and then I withdrew. Absorbed in my own need to carve space for myself, I'd been unable to sustain a semblance of communication. Four years later in the midst of the Tokyo lesbian community, I understood my fears as largely unwarranted. Listening to the horrifying story of the father who beat his daughter upon discovering a fax from the Tokyo Lesbian and Gay Parade organisers, I reinforced how much I'd over-calculated the distance I had established. Yet, in my moment of revelation, my desire to be honest required a sub-clause of escape. Tokyo symbolised more than that to me.

After three months living in Tokyo, I'd reassessed my pursuit of easy fame. Working at the model agency I began to understand more of the transient Japanese market. The greater contact I had with entertainment promotion, the more I knew I didn't want to be subjected to the tabloid media's unrelenting glare. I enjoyed working in the peripheries, and spent late hours at the agency. After work, I looked forward to spending time with Marou. Within a short time, my friend returned to Australia to be with his lover. With encouragement from Tokyo pals, I began to put myself first. I started rehearsing with Marou's band Kinbiren, and gushed rudimentary poems into my pocket writing pad. Now, sitting in this coffee shop I felt close to the energy of people surging down the hill. As I read through the letter from my father, I sensed a new step; the new beginnings of a mutual understanding which would require ongoing care.

Back in Perth for a year, I negotiated the new buildings in the city and began to reorient my emotions. Picking up where things left off is only easy if the point of departure is precise. Simply put, the Perth airport lobby was the final point where my family and friends had waved goodbye, yet to me it signalled nothing more than the port of my exit and re-entry. It was neither a link nor a chain. Any semblance of departure for me lay scattered over the skies. Sat nestled between the lines of letters and was caught in pauses carried over the telephone. Standing in the Perth airport carpark with Marou and Kelly, looking at the cobalt blue midnight sky, I was frightened. I wanted to make relationships anew, but was unsure how to shake my preconceptions from the past. After we moved from Nikki's to Northbridge, the twenty-dollar double bed we bought sat in the front room, functioning as my private symbol of rebellion. Its power waned the longer I spent time with my family in coffee shops outside.

Six months after Marou and I arrived in Perth, my eldest sister and her husband were expecting their first child. On the afternoon of the expected day I picked up the phone as it rang from the kitchen counter.

"It's a girl!" Mum screamed into my ear. Her excitement was infectious. I could feel myself bouncing. In my mind I ran through a list of florists where I could buy flowers. Suddenly the bouncing stopped. My mind computed the phrase "immediate family only". I carried on the rest of the conversation on remote control, wrote down directions to the ward and replaced the receiver. Slowly I walked into the study where Marou was working.

"What's wrong?"

"Sorry, only immediate family are allowed in the hospital room. Mum specifically said so."

My heart started to back-pedal and my pulse seemed to drop. I paced around our desks. Then turned to pace the other way.

"Maybe we should leave going until tomorrow?"

"Don't be so silly. Hurry up and go. I can go with you another time. The new mother's probably too tired to see anyone anyway. Get in the car and go."

I was surprised at how calm Marou appeared to be.

Before I knew it I was parking Ginga in the hospital carpark. I gathered the flowers in my arms and made my way up to the ward.

I checked the name on the door before I opened it. Sure enough, sitting up in bed was my sister. She looked tired, but amazingly happy. The beaming father was beside her. I tried not to concentrate on the sea of faces, but as she reached out to hug me I noticed that my brother's girlfriend at the time was standing to my left.

"Where's Marou?" my sister asked. I felt a twinge of pain poke at my chest.

Any words I had dried in my throat. Was I in the middle of some horrible misunderstanding? I glanced around me again: my brother-in-law's brother and his girlfriend were admiring the baby. I tried to be brave. I smiled. I reached over for my first hug but the longer I was in the room the more nauseous I felt. I made my excuses and closed the door behind me. Sadness and confusion made way for anger. I charged towards the elevator; a long stretch of blue carpet stared at me. I couldn't stand the hospital's claustrophobic atmosphere any more. All I wanted to was to make it home unnoticed.

The door of the elevator opened.

On the other side, champagne in hand, faces brimming with happy smiles, stood my parents.

"What's wrong?"

Streams of people entered the lobby. The elevator rocked in and out with the motion of people.

"I don't want to talk about it here" is all I could manage to say as I almost ran for the entrance. Outside I gasped for air. Just what had happened in there? Had I imagined it? Constructed it? Misheard? I faltered. I began to question. Suddenly I was nineteen years old and stranded on the university oval with only myself to pull me through a panic attack.

When I got home I couldn't face Marou; a thousand demons ran through my mind. I checked through every dictionary I could find.

"Stop it. It isn't your fault. It's nobody's fault."

Exhausted, we collapsed into each other's arms.

After three days of silence, I rang my mother. I knew I risked ruining a celebratory occasion, but I had to tell her what I had experienced if I was really going to renegotiate our relationship, which had always been close. Cutting myself off from Australia two and a half years ago had literally saved my life. Yet, after months here with Marou I'd actually begun to rediscover parts of this town I liked. Driving Ginga along the coast I discovered a remarkable sense of calm. Staring through the white gums into a brilliant blue sky soon eased any uneasy feelings I had. This land was more powerful than I had imagined. I needed to flesh it out with people, let myself slide back into the landscape. Coming out on the run had given us all time to adjust. Now I had to accept the responsibility of continuing the task. Saying the words was perhaps the easiest part, sharing the pain of understanding the ramifications of those words was by far the hardest.

I could hear Mum's surprise at my serious tone of voice.

"But darling, I never meant it like that. Of course Marou's part of the family."

I breathed a sigh of relief. That was all I needed to hear right now.

Too concerned about the reactions of others I had worked in collusion. Pain burned in my chest and I tried to search for a way to the open sky. I could hear my mother sigh and from the other end of the phone I felt her silence smile into my pain.

"We'll just have to work on it," was all that she said.

I began to feel seeds of reconciliation grow and a blue passage of the sky sparkled through the window, landing softly on my hand.

Chapter 6

HIGH SCHOOL

All of a sudden it was autumn. From the university library cafeteria I gazed out at the red of the turning leaves, the blue of the always bright sky, the green of the grass bending in the wind. Surrounded by trees, an invigorating shine of colours extended before the library.

Reading books, drinking coffee, chatting with members of the gay association, I used this magnificent building as I pleased. The red, blue and green scenery decorated a truly free and easy lifestyle of gazing out on time and relaxing under the brightly burning sun. By the standards of conservative society this would probably be dismissed as lazy. To me it was pure luxury which brought happiness beyond belief. According to Foucault, since the birth of modern commercial society and the banishment of "idleness", people have been encouraged into a busy lifestyle directed purely towards a life goal. We moderns have been educated from a young age to hold some sort of goal we must actively pursue. To those who have accepted that concept without question, the magnificent feeling of this relaxed pace would only signal the ingredients of instability.

Fortunately as a lesbian I was forced to question things in adolescence. Life achievement—ha! For me, the fundamental question was first, where did you say my place in this society was? The answer I repeatedly got? Nowhere.

At the time I thought there was nowhere in society lesbians could live as themselves. The only lesbian information found in the media was about Togawa Masako's lesbian bar the Blue Room. Scandals involving celebrities had made the bar famous, but the lesbian bar scene and living as you are seemed to be two very different things. I went to the abyss of despair and for a while wondered whether I should leap into it. I was right on the edge, but pulled back. There wasn't any one "thing" in particular, just an amazing force to survive. After pulling back I was fine. I could declare that everyone who rejects me because I'm different is wrong. Thanks to being forced into a minority position, I was able to see how society stuffed people into compartments and educated them for easy control.

The situation is the same for lesbian and gay children as it is for adults. Currently, lesbian and gay children are deprived daily of their freedom to not do what they don't want to do. "Show interest in the opposite sex." "Date the opposite sex." Now, as before, children are forcibly coerced into heterosexuality. It's always the "wants" in a person's life which take the spotlight, but actually *not* doing what you *don't* want to do is also extremely important.

I was surprised at the substantial number of healthy-looking Australian kids who apparently attempt suicide. One day Kelly came to our door looking very shocked and distressed. The brother of one of her friends had shot himself without leaving a note or anything. Nobody knew why. Kelly's distress started my mind spinning.

Suicide is not someone else's problem.

Youth suicide personally raises issues of sexuality for me. It's difficult for lesbian and gay teenagers to pass through the already unstable years of adolescence, especially because sexuality is an extremely vague entity at that time. Even at this young age, the world suppresses any sexuality perceived as differing from society's "majority rules" principle. Consequently, a person can develop the fear of losing the reason for their very existence. This fear is frighteningly real. Understandably, lesbian and gay surveys always include a question on attempted suicide experiences.

According to an article I read in Perth's gay and lesbian newspaper the *Westside Observer*, 30 percent of teenagers who attempt suicide do so due to problems with sexuality. A large number of gay men and lesbians are undoubtedly part of this figure. Yet this is only the number of people treated in hospitals. I imagine the actual suicides and attempts is much higher. Without doubt, those who can think of no way except death of *not doing what you don't want to do* are among those who suicide.

A heap of old memories surfaced as I listened to Kelly talk.

It was thirty years ago in lower high school.

The school siren had sounded. As I remember, we had not long returned from the annual school trip to Tokyo.

A huge red evening sun shone diagonally through the open classroom window. A group of close friends were still excited from four days visiting Tokyo Tower, the Imperial Palace and the Diet buildings. We made no attempt to head for home and, soaked in a romantic feeling, gazed at the sun. The frequency of utterances lessened. There was a feeling of wanting to be here forever, of melting into the view.

As if to destroy that delicious feeling, a lump of boredom who didn't know how to shut up spoke: "Let's all confess who we like."

Unfortunately high school kids soon flatter their friends. "Shut up! Don't you understand the beauty of silently melting into the view! Dickhead!" Words impossible to say.

I seethed with loathing for him on the inside. Yet, on the outside I jumped up and down playing *janken* to decide the order we would confess. A boy who'd been labelled as the smartest student enrolled since the founding of the school was the first to go. Bright red, he hesitantly said, "The person with the same hobby as me, the one who likes the Beach Boys."

In this boring country school the only people in the class who talked about the Beach Boys were him and me. The force of the genius's confession was amazing. "Yeow! uohh-uohhh!" Everyone was drawn straight into a whirlpool of excitement. Eventually kids who couldn't remain on their chairs started running around the room screaming.

What's more, he continued, "I noticed ages ago, at the school assembly when we were lined up in the gardens to practise the school song and national anthem. You were the only one who took no notice and refused to sing. Remember?" He spoke politely, the only boy in the class not to address girls by their last names or call them *omae*. "I hated having to practise some stupid song. It felt like the army. What with the teachers ordering us to 'Assemble!' and 'Attention!' I couldn't keep my eyes off you and just kind of grew to like you," he faded off.

Sharp. Too sharp. He was unable to see through the fact that I stood there not thinking of anything, just staring into space. Come to think of it, I didn't hate him. As a friend, someone to talk to, I liked him. But feelings of affection are without reason, without meaning. There is some chance moment, after which you are engulfed by the intention to "make you mine" and the storm and stress of passion breaks out.

I knew only too well the difference between *like* and *love*. My current theme was how to pull the reins on my own unreasonable, selfish, uncontrollable feelings. I had only ever felt *love* for one very special girlfriend. She was a being with amazing brightness. She changed freely at will. To me she was sometimes rival, sometimes best friend, sometimes fiendish lover, sometimes penfriend, sometimes counsellor, sometimes the most infuriating person on earth. She was also right there. By and by it was my turn.

That special girlfriend sat silently staring at me. Faced with the genius boy and my friend, I understood clearly, too clearly, the difference between liking as a friend and liking as in love. I wanted desperately to scream out her name, to name the name of the person staring straight at me. The genius boy flew right out of my mind.

"I can't say it, I can't say it, I can't say it!" I got redder. The more I stressed it, the more everyone got worked up.

"Who? Who?" Even she asked, knowing full well how I felt. "Why don't you say it? You've got some reason why you can't?"

"I can't say, can't say, can't say." After battling for over ten minutes, I was left with no way out. I mumbled the name of the genius boy.

"Ahhh! Perfect match!" Not satisfied with running around the classroom, everyone ran yelling down the hallway. "So how are you going to go on from here? Exchange diaries?" they screamed in excitement.

The lump of boredom ended by saying, "Feel free to come to me for advice."

My special girlfriend said, "That's great, you both like each other" in a totally unconcerned manner, then started talking about herself. She delightedly confessed the name of a boy so inconspicuous you hardly knew he was in the class.

I maintained an unconcerned exterior, but inside I was going berserk.

May she fall directly upside down into the deepest depth of hell!

Who cares if she likes someone else, I can handle it!

I wanted to let the person I really cared for know that I did. I didn't want to say I liked someone I didn't—especially not in front of the person I really did. That's all it was. I was placed in an inescapable position. This marked the beginning of my lesbian self being robbed of the small freedom not to do what I didn't want to do.

I didn't want people being surprised or teasing me about the one feeling of all that was most sacred to me. I didn't want to be hurt by people who knew nothing about a very special and dear emotion that even I didn't have a name for. I had heard of the word lesbian which circulated as a derogatory term for so-called "horrible mannish women". But it wasn't a name to come out of high-schoolers' mouths. For me, as one of those students, the thought of being treated as a curiosity was unbearable. Coming face to face with my reality frightened me the most.

Not matter how inconsequential this may seem to me now, it is the first major problem lesbian and gay youth experience as they grow into adults. Firstly, you surprise yourself at your own reality. Then, you realise that reality isolates you from others. Regardless, you refuse to talk about your reality for fear of isolation. In terms of sexuality, being forced into the minority is feeling this fear. If your clothes are different to everyone else's, then after a while you have the answer. After all, your style is always the grooviest. But lower high school is a difficult age for sexuality. Even adults keep it secret. The Japanese are under-handed about desire.

The pain of doing things I didn't want to do became heavier in upper high school. Even I panicked. I went on date after date with that genius boy from lower high school, an adultish senior boy from the basketball club, and a guy from a different school who whisked over to help when I fell ice skating; all the time wondering when the day I would feel romantically towards boys would come.

I never felt anything dazzling that made my heart pound, whoever the boy. No matter how happy they were to do things, it was only ever painful for me. Precious time was spent wasted. Why must I forever hang around with boys doing nothing when they don't make my pulse race? Why does there have to be some sort of sexual attraction just because it's a girl and a boy? I was severely attracted to girls. To me, sexual relations, sleeping together could only be on the other side of higher tension and hot desire, and I soon got angry that these "boyfriends" had the spare time to confuse nothing relationships with love. On the outside I pretended bravery, but between the years of lower and upper high school I felt like cinders drifting in a bottomless fake sky. I could do nothing but clam up about true feelings and desires.

One day my family and I were eating at the dinner table. Suddenly my mother inquired in a quiet but tense voice, "Is something wrong?"

I was surprised by her tone of voice. As I became aware of myself I noticed that I was staring into my rice bowl with tears flowing silently. My real desires were so completely different to everyone else's. That was the last I could stand of continually being at a loss about my feelings.

I never thought to ask for help. No matter how much I respected or trusted a person, I felt they wouldn't understand my true desire because they themselves were heterosexual. For a while, I didn't do anything but climb up onto the roof and gaze at the night sky, thinking. Maybe the earth was the only one among the thousands of stars inhabited by life forms. Maybe it wasn't. I turned my ears towards the nothingness of solitude and darkness. The universe spoke to me with amazing volubility. The light travelling across millions of light-years filled my darkness.

The real universe taught me more about society's falsities, more about the wonder of living true to your desires, than any half-baked psychoanalysis text.

I got over this heavy stage and was able to declare, "I'm never going to do what I don't want to, and I don't have to." For me going out with boys was not related to my own desire, it was society's hidden demand. Modern society cunningly pretends that everyone is free to do what they want, while actually coercing you into doing opposite.

Even in Perth, those who fall outside societal perimeters are harassed. The pressure to conform is great. In a society exerting such constant pressure, when individuals make choices at life's forked roads they don't select a path according to their individual needs, but as a result of society's coercion.

When I made the decision to live in Perth, friends worried strangely. "There's nothing to do in Perth, you'll be bored." To me, a lifestyle where you have to be always doing something or else you'll be bored is the most boring of all. In Perth I never grew tired of spending morning, day, night living with JJ. Perth is a very special place for me, a place etched deeply into my memory.

Living in Perth, after a day's work or study, JJ and I often went to watch the sun set into the Indian Ocean. They say that in the spring whales pass through this ocean joined to the South Arctic Sea. Brushed by the breeze blowing from the other side of the horizon, JJ and I talked. We never grew tired of talking about how life might develop. With JJ here with me, those childhood days when living as myself was so difficult, felt like a funny old story. The breeze surrounding me blew in from beyond the future sphere. Perth's autumn grew deeper in colour day by day.

Chapter 7

WATASHI, OTAMBI, DYKE

It is the middle of winter. I can now make my way around town, go to the gym, take in a coffee shop, browse at the bookstore. A group of Christians have recently taken to appearing at the crossing in front of the Arcane bookshop. They hand out flyers proclaiming "The Arcane is a house of sin" to people standing at the lights. Even the store's keyhole has been vandalised.

"Marou, face it, you're basically a vanilla dyke." JJ strolled past to see me reading *Wicked Women* inside.

"You scared me." I turned to JJ. "Hey, I've only ever heard of 'dyke', what's a 'vanilla dyke'?"

"Well, there's bulldog dykes and diesel dykes, which kind of puts the emphasis on strength. And vanilla dykes are like the name, sweet," JJ gently mocked.

Naming and language difference are big issues. Just ask JJ, she's got a special interest in differences in the Japanese language and their relation to women's position in Japanese society. Once she starts on the subject she goes on for hours.

In "correct Japanese" that "foreigners" like JJ are expected to learn, there are many words acceptable for men to use to women but not for women to use to men. A good example is the informal second-person pronoun *omae* (you), which many language teachers explain as appropriate for men to use to women. Put simply, tuition in "correct Japanese" gives learners the covert message that men are superior to women in Japanese-language relationships.

Around the time JJ started to really complain about being taught "correct Japanese" at university, a friend who'd seen the film version of Yoshimoto Banana's *Tsugumi* sent a postcard saying, "Marou, Tsugumi is the spitting image of you as a child." I don't know whether she meant that I was a horrible kid (the main character Tsugumi is a bit of a brat), but I do know for sure that I tried my best to refuse "women's language" and as a child spoke a lot of "men's language", like Tsugumi.

In English, whether one is a woman or a man, working-class or middle-class, there is only the one word "I" to express oneself. For men in Japanese there are the first-person pronouns *boku*, *ore*, *washi*, *watashi* and so on to choose from, depending on the speaker's social status in relation to the addressee. For women, however, the range is generally limited to *watashi*.

There is a big gap between the me that is "Marou" and the *watashi* that women are expected to use. I wasn't able to bring myself to use *watashi* for a long time. As soon as I even pronounced it I'd be overcome with the feeling that the person in question wasn't really me. "Women's language" enforces the concept that women in Japan are either non-individuals or continuously humble towards others. Using "men's language" didn't mean I wanted to be a man, just that I wanted to express myself directly. To untie yourself from superior/subordinate relationships and express yourself frankly, the natural choice is direct language. Unfortunately, this is also classified as "men's language". Maybe refusing the "women's word" *watashi* had something to do with my being a lesbian, but I think unconsciously rejecting "the 'I' that means female" was more a result of the desire to be myself. Nowadays it's not so unusual for girls to use "men's language" like the character Tsugumi does, or for boys to use *watashi*, but when I was a kid over three decades ago? Being born ahead of the times has a kind of excitement, but it sure does make for a lot of wasted time.

It was the height of the 1970s.

Tōgō Ken was the mainstay of the gay group Zatsumin no Kai (the Association of Miscellaneous People), and regularly stood for municipal and parliamentary seats. In the lead-up to elections, the national broadcasting commission NHK allocated a few minutes to each candidate. Tōgō Ken deliberately spoke provocatively during his allotted time.

"I am Tōgō Ken, the faggot. Listen to me carefully everyone. The emperor boy could do with a prick up his ass." In three minutes full of words prohibited for broadcasting, he would say all the things he usually couldn't. Although people around me discussed his comments, Tōgō Ken never attracted enough votes for a seat. His general politics were unclear. Plans went ahead, however, to produce an underground gay-lib theatre piece starring Tōgō Ken himself.

On the streets, underground theatre was gaining popularity. The performers, producers and audiences of both musicals and commercial productions staged in large theatres, and medium-sized performances of classic Shakespeare and Chekhov, had stalled into monotonous repetition during the thirty years since the war. As if to overthrow the stuffy scene, underground theatre companies sprang up prolifically during the 1970s. The most famous of these were Jōkyō Gekijō and Tenjō Sajiki. For these groups with no money or fame, the context of a theatre world which would not allow them to rent performance space was itself a medium of expression. They erected giant tents and performed in temple grounds, in parks and on abandoned construction sites without permits. They incorporated the actions of the riot police who came to evict them, and the curiosity seekers who watched, into the stories performed on stage. They succeeded in creating breathtakingly dramatic spaces by making liberal use of fire, oil and water; materials prohibited for use in commercial theatres by fire regulations.

Performers from the underground tent theatres gradually became popular with office workers. Radical theatre groups became absorbed as a form of trendy entertainment, and were transformed as a result of changing audiences.

The gay-lib underground performance of *Kaiten Doa no Mukō no Umi* (The Ocean beyond the Revolving Door) was produced by and starred Tōgō Ken. It boasted an impressive line-up of staff. Dōmoto Masaki, a theatre critic specialising in *Kabuki* and *Noh*, who was also a scriptwriter close to Mishima Yukio, wrote the script. Music was composed by Saegusa Nariaki, who, although unknown at the time, went on to achieve fame as a composer in the 1980s. Yotsuya Shimon, the famous doll artist who was also popular as a drag queen in Jōkyō Gekijō performances, was in charge of make-up. Actors included Tanuko, who performed with Jōkyō Gekijō, Mitchan from the bar Forest of Fire, the *Mama* of Club France (all big stars from the gay bar scene), and actors from Roman Theatre who had scattered after Mishima Yukio's death.

A group of young actors influenced by writer Mishima Yukio formed the short-lived and barely known Roman Theatre around the time Mishima shifted his interests from literature to film and dramatic expression. However, in November 1970, Mishima and members of his private army burst into the Self-Defence Force facilities in Ichigaya brandishing Japanese swords, and took the Inspector-General hostage. Mishima and Morita Hisshō, one of the men under Mishima's command, committed suicide by selfdisembowelment in the Self-Defence Force building. Roman Theatre disbanded shortly after.

At the time I was a non-political "gay woman" who spent most of my time shut up at home reading; I had no direct connection to any of these people. I just happened to be a friend of a friend of a friend of one of the organisers and was asked to play the lesbian role. I had never acted, never seen a play, wasn't interested in theatre. I took on the role because rather than having some clueless actor do a horrible job playing a lesbian image, I thought it'd be better if I acted naturally.

When strict rehearsals for the song-and-dance routine to music by Saegusa Nariaki began, my thinking towards Takarazuka, whose performance I'd always dismissed as being total nonsense, took a 180-degree turn. Takarazuka, the popular women's musical theatre company, was originally formed as the Takarazuka Girls Revue Theater Company in 1913. The owner of the Hankyū corporation, Kobayashi Ichizō, formed the revue as a means of attracting customers to the company's hot spring. Takarazuka has been wildly popular with its, mostly female, fans ever since. Stars who specialise in playing only male roles are popular with women of all ages and from all walks of life. If you like gaudy costumes and set design, the razzle-dazzle of Disneyland or Las Vegas, then Takarazuka may be for you. To me, Takarazuka was like a sickly-sweet sweet, made of nothing but sugar. I soon discovered, though, that to sing, dance and say lines is a big deal even in underground theatre. After singing and dancing and saying lines with her girlfriend who was still high school age, my lesbian character had to embrace her and act out a long kiss scene centre stage. For the duration of rehearsals, my acting partner and I made it look as if we were kissing when we actually weren't.

At the final dress rehearsal, the director, who hadn't said anything about the kiss scene throughout weeks of rehearsals, suddenly complained. "Make sure you really kiss during performances! Tongues twisted, a deep kiss, okay! Long, as loooong as you can. 'Are they still going, are they still going?', you've got to really provoke the audience into looking!"

The girl playing opposite and I had got our timing down during rehearsals and stood staring blankly at each other. We soon shook out of it. "Right, in performances. Okay."

"Yeah, the twisted tongues thing."

"Break a leg." We decided to give it our best.

Opening night. Who could have predicted it, a full house and no space left in the standing-only section.

My girlfriend, whom I'd been with for five years since university, was there with my friends. She was the eldest in an all-girl family, an accredited master of the Hanayagi school of *Nihon buyō* (Japanese dance), and was in charge of a small business in training to take over the family company. She was a hard-working, high-earning, Chanel-suited woman who sped over Tokyo's midnight freeways in her BMW to meet me nearly every night. She snuck out to see me because her family was suspicious of her relationship with me—they were right in their suspicions. You'd think sneaking out of the house late at night would make it more obvious. Maybe her family's intention was to tolerate things as long as she was secretive, thinking, "She'll get married eventually anyway."

There are limits to that kind of deception. At the time she had a special company post and all her material needs met, so was consequently torn daily between the choice of abandoning blood ties and employment to take me, her female lover, or marrying a man who would take on her surname as her parents wanted. Marrying such a man would ensure a more luxurious life than she now had.

"If I leave home and throw away family and work and Nihon buyō, will you stay with me for life?" She checked with me numerous times.

Each time I said, "I can't promise anyone anything for the future. Why should I take on the whole of your life?" It irked me considerably. Rather than understanding her situation of being threatened by parents into making a choice, I was angry at her lack of will to live independently. My head was full of the underground gay-lib theatre project and I didn't realise how far she had been cornered.

The curtain went up.

As to be expected, this underground group was a mess; we were far from professional actors. From before the curtain went up, actors were shouting, "If I don't have a drink I'll get stage fright in front of such a huge audience." A two-litre bottle of sake was passed around the dressing room.

Dressed in courtesan style, Tōgō Ken sounded like a drunk speaking his lines as he appeared from the raised stage passage running through the auditorium. The audience loved it. Bouquets of flowers flew from the auditorium during the scene where we all sang and danced, and my stage partner and I acted out a long, long kiss which in a moment quietened the audience into a breathless silence.

My girlfriend was waiting for me with friends after the curtain went down. We noisily walked down the street, but the instant someone said, "That kiss scene was long" my girlfriend suddenly gasped, and burst out crying. Throwing her bag and everything she carried down onto the bitumen, she ran off down the dark night road. Apparently that very day she had told her parents she would marry one of the arranged marriage partners they had lined up for her. As if to say "Hurry, before she changes her mind!", her parents had already confirmed the ceremony date and reception centre. I was the only one who didn't know about this matter of momentous importance.

Even after the play had finished its run, and we were back to the pattern of her speeding over the freeway in the middle of the night, it took a long time for her to tell me she had decided to marry. She looked as if she had something to say. "What's the matter?" I would ask, but "Oh, nothing. It's okay" was her only reply. Having been together so long, it was plain to me that she had something to say but couldn't.

Learning the truth from her only three weeks before the wedding, I was deeply shocked, and wild with anger. I didn't think about the possible consequences. I could only think of running away from the wedding that was bearing down in front of my eyes. We decided to "elope", to run away to Kyoto the next week. We planned to meet on the bullet train platform; to get away from work, she would pretend she was meeting clients then rush to Tokyo station.

It happened to be Aoi Festival time in Kyoto. Never before or since have I experienced walking through the bustling streets of Shijō in such depression. We finally settled down at a big hotel near Nijō castle, but we had both lost trust in each other and days of opening our mouths only to yell at one another continued.

These dark, bad-feeling days, however, soon came to a simple end.

I was woken by a forceful knock on the hotel room door just a few days later. Suspecting the worst, I opened the door with the safety chain still hooked up. Two plain-clothes police detectives flashed their identification and said, "We have words to say with her."

"Okay," she said from across the room and walked over to open the door.

"Your parents are very worried about you, they'll be arriving at Kyoto police headquarters soon. Please come with us immediately." The plainclothesmen spoke and pulled at her hand to take her with them.

"Wait a minute! You're an adult over twenty. You don't have to go if you don't want to," I screamed.

"If you say one more word we will arrest you for obstructing a government official in the course of his duties." The plainclothes detective standing between her and me spoke sharply. I was silenced by fear. I discovered later that, pressured by her parents, the police smelt out our hotel by searching my apartment and telephoning the workplaces of friends listed in the address book I had left at home in my rush.

Of course the elopement got back to my family.

My mother trusted me and, despite being bedridden, tried to pacify my girlfriend's parents who were worried we would commit a double "lovers'" suicide.

"Please don't worry. She isn't the kind to commit double suicide. If you just wait a little longer I'm sure they'll be in contact." She acted as the breakwater to parents who had fallen into a severe panic.

The wedding ceremony was called off.

The next ceremony was soon arranged.

Under familial observation since being brought back from Kyoto, my girlfriend escaped by jumping out the window and sped in a taxi to see me one night.

Utterly exhausted, we eloped for the second time. This second time was a desperate farce. She ran off, leaving me alone. I returned to my apartment fatigued and depressed, only to receive threatening phone calls from her parents.

"Don't think you can get away with it just because you're a girl. We have a Japanese sword in the house, you know."

"Oh? A Japanese sword? More importantly, has she been home?"

"You are the one who knows where our daughter is. Tell us where she is!"

"I don't know, that's why I'm asking. She hasn't been home? What am I going to do?"

"Liar!" And I heard the slam of the phone.

Two days later, my girlfriend told me personally that a friend had accompanied her home. I was exhausted with worry, didn't have the energy to do anything, no food would pass my throat. I slept like I'd collapsed. She suddenly appeared, like a zombie risen from the dead, only looking happy and carrying a supermarket shopping bag.

"What on earth are you doing here?"

"You probably haven't eaten, so I thought I'd make *sukiyaki*. I'll go as soon as I've made it. I slipped out secretly so I haven't much time."

"What? What are you thinking? Your wedding is the day after tomorrow, isn't it?"

"After I get married I'll come and see you, just forgive me for a little while. I'll come and see you as soon as I get back from the honeymoon."

I couldn't believe my ears. "Shit! You've got to be joking!" I took her spare key and shoved her and the shopping bag out the door. I can't lie around like this, I have to pick myself up. I have to get rid of the cause of this sickening chain of events. I went home for two weeks to rebuild my strength and sort out the incident. Mother didn't say anything, just offered kindness to my obviously tired, thinning self.

Just before I'd gone into rehearsals for the play, a lesbian activist for women's liberation sent me a questionnaire via a friend from university. It was the first questionnaire I'd ever seen made by lesbians for lesbians. I wrote in very small writing over both sides of the paper and a couple of days later I got a phone call. Because my answers were unique they wanted me to attend the discussion group.

The discussion group was held at the later abolished Lib Shinjuku Centre—commonly known as Libsen. At Libsen, I met about ten women who were like no-one I'd ever met before. It was the first time I'd ever met lesbian feminists who proclaimed "Lesbians are wonderful."

"You can't just run so quickly and say women are wonderful. I've been fighting alone since I was very little and there's so much of me that's been hurt." The lesbian feminists had no idea how to react to my jumbled opinions built on personal history. The ideas the lesbian feminists had imported from the United States dazzled, but seemed nothing more than experiments in trial and error which were unintelligible to me. Basically, I had culture shock.

"What's come out?"

"Sisterhood, ha. So you call it sibling love."

"Monogamous. Who … I am?"

"Could you please explain more clearly?"

This discussion group was the beginning of the first lesbian feminist magazine in Japan, *Subarashii Onnatachi* (Wonderful Women).

There were huge gaps between us but, as a result of being at that meeting, I wrote some articles, made the block to print the magazine, opened a post office box and did the rounds of stores who would stock underground magazines, all while having heated discussions with other members about feminism. Stubborn me couldn't understand the basic feminist thought of "grasping history and society from woman's point of view" without some struggle. At that time I insolently thought that I was special, that I had been brought up in a special home, that I had nothing in common with other, average, women. I was on the same "woman-hating" circuit toward women as many men in the world. I discovered misogyny was a feminist word.

Since childhood, I'd questioned the way I was educated "because you're a girl" by rejecting that idea outright. I said no, "because I don't want to". I didn't feel the problems of women who had never questioned social assumptions were any concern of mine. In fact, I despised them. I escaped becoming a totally non-objective and narcissistic *otambi* (an aesthete), however, through meeting these lesbian feminists and the elopement incident. The elopement to Kyoto destroyed the guard I had stubbornly set up against the world. It persuaded me that to live in this world I must accept all the general societal issues that were impossible to avoid as concerning me. That despising them and turning my back on them would achieve nothing.

The two weeks I spent at home were the turning point for me; this moderate non-political gay woman woke up to the lesbian feminist viewpoint. I came to understand my cultural, historical, and social positioning as a gay woman and woman. I also saw that the things I ate daily, hormone secretions, the direction of wind-blown pollen, today's weather, television commercials, the work of people called artists, explosions of new stars, demonstrations, the wars going on overseas were all related to me.

Until all women are liberated, there will be no liberation for lesbians.

I've talked about this with JJ. Halfway through her university year here in Perth, she's taken up classes apart from Japanese in "gender" and "women's studies" and has borrowed a huge number of lesbian feminist writings from the library. She reads right into the middle of the night, and I'm lullabied by explanations of post-modern feminism. Considering that when I first met her she called herself a "gay woman" and said "I don't like the words lesbian or dyke very much", this is a very big change. She's even begun to think of studying more about Japan, polishing her skills to work towards making a liberated society where lesbians can live boldly. Her new aim is to get into university in Japan.

Lesbian existence contains many possibilities that shake not only contemporary society, which takes heterosexuality as universal, but also male-centred culture. The reality of women being sexually attracted to women is beyond explanation. Make-up, clothing, fashion—neither JJ nor I can accept without question the beauty values men have forced onto women. Nonetheless, it's not only men who find a beautiful woman beautiful. Love and desire between women exists in a place unrelated to androcentric society and takes no account of men.

I'll keep referring to myself as gay woman, lesbian, dyke, as the mood and circumstances find me.

Chapter 8

TOKYO CLOSETS

Love

I arrived in Tokyo tired and emotionally stunned. Leaving Perth was difficult. In one short year I'd built confidence to survive in my birth city. Marou had opened my eyes to the depth of Perth's open skies, reacquainted me with the soothing qualities of eucalypt bark. She'd been alongside as I re-established a relationship with my family which was neither threatening nor angry. She'd become a friend to my friends. Waving goodbye to them all from the departure lobby at Perth airport, I was overwhelmed by tears I didn't want to share. After my ten-hour solo journey I was glad to re-enter the congested smells of Narita airport.

My direct flight touched down mid-morning. Exiting customs, I scanned the arrival hall. Dreary airport chairs floated in my field of vision.

"It is so good to see you." Marou was standing near the flight information monitor. "My flight was horrible. The stopover in Malaysia was gruelling. I don't ever want to do that again. Next time you get a scholarship, make sure they offer to book a plane ticket for your partner too, hey." Marou's laughing hands soothed my shoulders, but I pulled back. Her words reminded me that this flight home was the beginning of a year studying under scholarship at a Tokyo university. I glanced furtively around the lobby to locate the scholarship foundation's arrival committee. Huddled beside a potted plant was a woman with a clipboard. My name and room allocation were undoubtedly part of her day's agenda.

"The Perth people wouldn't listen when I said I didn't need accommodation. Wait here, I'll go and talk to the arrival committee now." The scholarship provided a monthly stipend and a room in the university dormitory. No matter how small, no matter that you could hear the person next door turning in their sleep, the promise of a room in central Tokyo was not something to be pushed aside nonchalantly. Metropolitan property owners could demand up to a total of four months' rent in advance. Some even required prospective occupants to supply financial documents for a personal guarantor. Marou and I had plans to return to sharing our one-room apartment with Nyan Nyan. Before anything, I had to cancel the university dorm room.

Walking alone across the arrival lobby, a strangely familiar pressure invaded my conscious mind. The closet. I was back in my Tokyo closet.

Crossing at the lights near Kichijōji station I was welcomed by the smell of hot noodle soup. Despite the normality of illegally parked bicycles scattered across the pavement outside the *rāmen* shop, something felt different. The usually fast-paced Tokyoites were dragging their feet. Falling real estate prices, company restructuring. Newspaper headlines I'd read on the plane screamed out news of a recession—the bubble had apparently burst. Regardless of the gloomy headlines, a new cram school had materialised on the corner of our block. Groups of high school students leaked onto the footpath to catch their breath between lessons in their academic fight for university entry. Shaking my head at the fake brick exterior, I walked the next thirty metres to our room with Marou.

"Nyan Nyan, we're home." Marou called while I slipped my shoes off at the front door.

Coolly restrained in her greeting, Nyan Nyan sat stubbornly in the centre of the wooden floor. Her eyes didn't actually focus on me; she let them run past my feet two or three times. Now I knew I was home. After a year's absence our apartment appeared even smaller and more cosy. Marou's desk faced the railway line, an arm's length away from where mine stood nestled between the bathroom door and closet. Nyan Nyan lazily pushed against my legs demanding fish flakes. Her back shone as she slowly approached her bowl by the fridge.

"Looks like it's back to sharing my *nori* with you, hey," I smiled.

At the foreign students' orientation session a week later, nearly fifteen of us sat around an oval table. We politely smiled as we passed along the campus handbook, the library guide, a thin *How to Survive in Japan* booklet. The old campus rooms were badly heated and I made a mental note to buy some warm underwear. The formality which crept up my back pushed into my mind. I couldn't grin and say, "Yes, I just got home a couple of weeks ago, Tokyo's changed in the last twelve months, hey." I couldn't introduce a Japanese wife or husband who might provide an explanatory interface for my Tokyo attachment. I was labelled; single, white, female, straight, foreigner—a temporary resident so flighty it was unsure just when I might up and off home. Like the other foreign students in this room, I needed a visa to stay, a thumbprinted alien registration card to prove my legality, and re-entry permits if I ever wanted to holiday overseas. I fought the temporary, the foreign, but it took me two years to get the "heterosexual single" label out of my university garb.

Lectures started mid-April. "Making friends" was a concept almost impossible to enact. My initial lack of specialist knowledge also made it difficult to engage in discussion. In preparation for my classes, I spent hours decoding the required reading, only to have long swirls of ancient script dance unintelligibly before me during tutorials.

"I'm sorry, I don't understand," I mumbled to my academic supervisor who had asked me to explain a section of text.

"Ms J. Don't apologise. You have only just begun. Give yourself time." He nodded, light from the old fluorescent shining on his balding head.

My lack of expertise I could handle, but the time it took to log into the information exchange system was excruciating. Regulatory health checks, registration deadlines—I stood for long minutes in front of the notice boards, trying to gather information everyone else seemed to catch on the wind. The colossal library system was a sleeping dinosaur. When I finally found the gender theory book I was searching for buried in one of the law libraries, the librarian informed me that, not being a law student myself, it was impossible for me to borrow it even with a letter of introduction from my department. Every step on campus weighed me down.

"What happened this time?" Marou asked as I sobbed down the receiver.

"I asked the computing centre about Japanese-language concordance programmes. They told me to learn how to write computer programmes before bothering them again. My tutor doesn't know what I'm talking about and I don't know who else to ask." The highlight of my daily routine was telephoning Marou.

A month of campus life and I had an updated inventory of frequently asked questions.

"Where do you live? In the university dorm?" a fellow student in my lexicology class asked.

"Um, no. I live in an apartment." I smiled knowing what would come next.

"An apartment? Gee. By yourself? … No? … So, how much do you pay?"

New acquaintances first established where I lived, before moving onto my rent, the food I cooked and how I handled the shopping.

"Can you eat *miso* soup?" I replied deadpan to another domestic query. Unfortunately, turning the questions around only resulted in quizzical stares.

Non-reciprocal questioning wasn't new to me. As an exchange student in high school I'd had my lifestyle scrutinised, my behaviour on public show, yet, since I was no longer part of a host family or enacting a traditional family, I was made aware of limits I'd never experienced before. My coping strategy was to withdraw—politely. I was easy to get along with, efficacious. I manoeuvred around personal questions without actually lying. In the department room I was full of smiles. Attending every class I could, I used the dictionary collection to pull me through the maze of classical Japanese. Lunchtime phone-box chats with Marou emotionally pulled me through my regime of classes.

Privileges threatened me and, as Marou and I became more involved in the increasingly vocal off-campus queer community, the scholarship clause prohibiting political activities photocopied larger and larger in my mind. I talked in interviews as a lesbian, but under a pseudonym. I was out to family, friends, the doctor who did my pap smears, yet I deliberately created a cheerful distance on campus to avoid personal interactions. A paranoiac state of confused politics. The possibility of disaster silenced me. I'd lost my visa once before. Losing it again was a fear too real to negate.

Chapter 9
GOLDEN WEEK

"I know. Let's go to the Yoshiya Nobuko Memorial Museum," JJ said as if she'd come up with an amazing idea.

It was the holiday week in May. Golden Week, stretching from the end of April to the first week of May, is the biggest vacation period in Japan next to New Year. North to Hokkaido, south to Okinawa, even overseas; theme parks, concerts, theatres, cinemas, sports grounds, shopping centres and restaurants are crowded with flocks of Japanese people.

JJ had commenced as a research student at the classical Japanese-language department of a Tokyo university, and *what* to do during these holidays was her current concern. A year away from Japan, refreshing weather; JJ was bursting to go somewhere. As for me, book preparations had lulled and it wasn't as if I didn't have time to play. Still, I didn't especially want to walk around and participate in the infamous Golden Week crowds.

"But we've just come back to Japan. I want to go somewhere over the break."

"Over Golden Week? Everywhere's crowded."

"Hey, so what?"

"The trains, they're all full."

"Hey, that's okay."

"No way. There's masses of people everywhere."

"Hey, so how about the Yoshiya Nobuko Memorial Museum?"

My determination not to go anywhere over the holiday was swayed by JJ's one comment.

Yoshiya Nobuko (1896–1973) is the most famous and successful closeted lesbian writer in Japan. From 1916 she wrote serials for magazines. Her early representative work *Hana monogatari* (Flower stories)[1] was wildly popular with adolescent girls in the Taishō era and created a new genre in popular fiction known as "girls' fiction".

An extremely popular writer, Yoshiya Nobuko and her secretary Monma Chiyo (1899–1988) are, so to speak, the Japanese Gertrude Stein and Alice B. Toklas.

It was one day of the holiday.

JJ and I took the JR line from Tokyo station about an hour to Kamakura, transferred to the Enoshima Dentestu line and got off at a rustic station called Hase. The weather was clear. It was the beginning of a lovely day. Crowds of people formed a line extending to the famous Giant Buddha. Walking off from the road to the Giant Buddha, which had been transformed into a target destination for the mass relocation of Japan's heterosexual, coupled population, we breathed a sigh of collective relief. Presently, a splendid gateway appeared enclosed by a wooden fence. Inside was the former Yoshiya residence. Middle-aged men formed a belt cleaning around the entrance. They wore suits with name bands which made them look like tired public servants.

"Ah-hum. The Yoshiya Nobuko Memorial House is presently open for special inspection. Welcome. All are welcome." One or two called out and approached tourists trying to pass by the gateway. A few of the straight couples they approached stopped

[1] First serialised in *Shojō gahō* (1916–24).

with a "hmmph". "Well, shall we go in?" they whispered to each other, then passed through the main gates of the museum.

A bad feeling grazed somewhere across my mind. My eyes met JJ's. "Ahh——" A sigh leaked from her lips; JJ had a similar hunch. We hadn't counted on such a huge crowd of tourist couples. I had expected more of the visitors to be interested in Yoshiya Nobuko.

A Japanese-style timber house stood majestically beyond the wooden door of the main gateway, deep in the interior of a vast Japanese garden. The straight couples sitting along the long semi-enclosed verandah facing onto the garden looked like tiny beans. On the other side of the verandah was a living room separated by a transparent glass door. Another wooden gate led to the garden at the end of a stone path running immediately from the entrance. JJ and I stood peeking onto the landscape through a gap in the wooden gate.

"Ah-hum. You can't enter the garden through there. Don't stop, follow the route directly ahead to the entrance. At the entrance please take off your shoes." A public service worker raised his voice at the main gate. He'd been waiting to seize that one brief moment when JJ and I stopped at the small gate to view the interior garden.

Looking closer I saw a message posted on the gate. "No entrance from this point."

"I understand. I can read. We're just looking. Don't hassle me just because I'm a *gaijin*." JJ's voice was rough. The public service worker's head disappeared behind the main gate.

The entrance was a storm of caution signs.

"Take off your shoes here. No removing shoes elsewhere." "Here" was the point before the entrance where a plank had been laid down to form a path.

"Under all circumstances place your shoes on the shoe racks."

"Please wear slippers."

"Toilet this way."

"There is enough paper stuck up here to make a book." Exasperated, I stepped into the building. Inside the living room, rows of photo panels covered the walls. In the photos Yoshiya Nobuko was smiling with the crown prince, with the prime minister, with army officers, politicians, a movie director, film stars, famous writers of the period. Nobuko looked very much like a butch dyke with an unflattering but highly fashionable bobbed hairstyle, unusually short for women at the time. Dressed in chic suits with huge shoulder pads and skirts which I didn't think suited her, she stood firmly with feet apart, mouth wide open, laughing freely.

"Hmph. So what?" In spite of myself my lip curled up. Chiyo wasn't even in the private photo taken with a group of close women friends.

"It can't be …" JJ hurriedly read the people listed at the bottom of the photo panels name by name. "Here." At last she found Chiyo's name. She was at the edge of a group photo of about ten or more people. Positioned far away from Nobuko, who was grinning in the middle of the group, it was as if Chiyo had no close relationship with Nobuko whatsoever.

"Great writer and her secretary, huh?"

"Huh!"

"Nobuko and Chiyo didn't do women's rights campaigning or participate in ideological activism, but they sure were special," JJ almost whispered, as if to regain composure.

True, Nobuko hadn't participated in any form of organised political activity. Yet, in an era when it was difficult merely for women to work, with Chiyo's cooperative efforts, Nobuko became a highly successful writer who received great public support—especially from young women.

Yoshiya Nobuko and Monma Chiyo first met in January 1923. Yamataka Shigeri, who went on to be a well-known suffragist, introduced her close friend Chiyo to Nobuko, who was negative about "women's friendships". Shigeri thought highly of her friendship with Chiyo, a young woman who had chosen to remain unmarried and worked to support her elderly parents in what were difficult circumstances for a woman at that time in Japan. Yoshiya Nobuko, then twenty-seven years old, was the author of *Hana monogatari* (Flower tales),[1] *Yane ura no ni shojo* (Two virgins in the garret),[2] and *Chi no hate made* (To the end of the earth).[3] She and Chiyo, a 23-year-old mathematics teacher, soon became lovers. In 1926, three years after their initial meeting, they commenced a collaborative working relationship as writer and secretary. Nobuko went on to publish *Onna no yūjō* (Women's friendships),[4] *Onna no kaikyū* (Women's social class),[5] and *Otto no teisō* (A husband's chastity).[6] She paid higher income tax than any other woman writer in 1935—a ranking that indicates her phenomenal success.

Nobuko began her career writing sugary girls' fiction and gradually developed her position as an established fiction writer. She successfuly produced popular fiction throughout the years before, during and after the war. Nobuko also published non-fiction, such as the anti-prostitution series *Toki no Koe* (Voice of time, 1964–65) in the *Yomiuri* newspaper. In her later years, she

[1] Serialised 1916–24.
[2] Tokyo: Rakuyōdō, 1920.
[3] Serialised in *Ōsaka Asahi Shinbun* during 1920.
[4] Serialised from 1933 in *Fujin Club*.
[5] Serialised in *Yomiuri Shinbun* during 1936.
[6] Serialised in *Tokyo Nichinichi Shinbun* during 1936.

turned her interests to women's history and created a new style of historical fiction with her novels *Tokugawa no Fujintachi* (The ladies of Tokugawa),[1] and *Nyonin Heike* (The ladies of Heike).[2]

For fifty years, Monma Chiyo supported Nobuko's work as her secretary and life companion. Chiyo attended to Nobuko's domestic chores, submitted her tax returns, entertained guests, coordinated annual celebratory events, walked her beloved pet dog, drove her car, prepared drafts for her speaking engagements. When Nobuko fell ill, Chiyo devoted time to nursing her. In her diary, Nobuko continually expressed sincere thanks for the happiness her partnership with Chiyo had brought, and for Chiyo's unending love and support. The following are segments from Nobuko's diary:

> Chiyo, on your birthday, I give thanks to fate which gave this person to me.
> Life happiness because of Chiyo.[3]

On 11 July 1973, almost a year after this entry, 77-year-old Nobuko died in a Kamukura hospital. Chiyo was at her side. The following day, Chiyo was interviewed by the press: "I, too, will die soon. Even in her old age, Ms Yoshiya remained in pursuit of the sweet fragrance of her girlhood dreams. Perhaps that is what attracted me. The passing of fifty years is, perhaps, merely one lady's dream."[4]

---

[1] Tokyo: Asahi Shinbunsha, 1966.
[2] Tokyo: Asahi Shinbunsha, 1971.
[3] Quoted in *Yoshiya Nobuko: Kakure Feminisuto* (Yoshiya Nobuko: closeted feminist), Komashaku Kimi, Tokyo: Riburopōto, 1994).
[4] *Mainichi Shinbun*, 12 July 1974. Quoted in *Yume Haruka Yoshiya Nobuko* (Distant dreams Yoshiya Nobuko), Tanabe Seiko, Tokyo: Asahi Shinbunsha, 1999, p. 559.

In the vast quantity of work Yoshiya Nobuko left behind, one finds a lively poem praising women, not ideologies and theories. The relationship, which made possible the voluminous work Nobuko and Chiyo bequeathed to Japanese popular fiction, differs markedly from the two other famous same-sex-love incidents which occurred during the same period in Japan.

These other famous female couples are Hiratsuka Raichō (1886–1971) and Otake Kōkichi (Kazue) (1893–1966); and Nakajō (Miyamoto) Yuriko (1899–1951) and Yuasa Yoshiko (1896–1990). They are known for their historical and famous literary love relationships between women in modern Japan.

Hiratsuka Raichō was the so-called founder of the Japanese women's rights movement. Her love affair with the hope of Japanese art, Otake Kōkichi, is so famous that in her later years Raichō desperately glossed over it in her autobiographical writings. Despite Raichō's efforts, however, it lies unerasable, merrily decorating one page of Japanese women's history.

Raichō and Kōkichi first met in April 1912. Raichō, twenty-six years old at the time, had studied as one of the elite of the elite at Japan's first women's university. It was fashionable for young intellectuals in the early 1900s to read philosophical works and the Bible; Raichō was also training in Zen and working daily towards self-enlightenment. Striving for self-improvement through Zen and philosophy on the one hand, Raichō was nonetheless deeply troubled by her social inferiority as a woman. She eventually began publishing the women-only magazine *Seitō* (Blue-stocking), with the purpose of "urging an awakening, and displaying women's individual natural talent with the aim of one day giving birth to woman genius", as she delared in the first issue in 1911. This art and literature magazine became the pioneer of modern Japanese women's rights.

Otake Kōkichi, aged nineteen, appeared before Raichō. Kōkichi was the eldest daughter of Otake Etsudō, a great master of Japanese painting. Without a traditional heir, Etsudō had raised his eldest daughter as a substitute son, destined to take over his work and carry on the family name. Raichō wrote about Kōkichi in *Genshi, josei wa taiyō de atta*.

> In complete men's drag of patterned *kimono* and over trousers or stiff *obi* and leather sandals, Kōkichi, cutting the air as she walks, saying what she wants to say, laughing and singing in a loud voice, displays true freedom and extravagance. The feeling of a person liberated since birth. Merely gazing upon her is pleasure.[1]

Raichō called Kōkichi "my boy" and their love apparently burst into flames immediately. The relationship was common knowledge among the other members of the *Seitō* staff. Indeed, until the establishment of US army bases nationwide after the Second World War when an excessive hetero-couple culture was imported, romantic crushes were common between women in Japan. Girls' fiction, the new genre established by Yoshiya Nobuko, was feverishly accepted as a result of this fertile soil.

Having found a wonderful lover in Raichō, Kōkichi ecstatically took charge of designing *Seitō*'s cover page and also began to produce essays. The cover of the April 1912 issue of *Seitō*[2] features a woodblock print designed by Kōkichi. A large black sun rises above a jar printed with the words "Blue Stocking" in English. In the next issue Kōkichi explained that the black jar was from a magical land: "The holder of the jar could use any strength or weakness at their will. However, no-one

---

[1] *Genshi, josei wa taiyō de atta* (In the beginning, women were the sun), Hiratsuka Raichō, Tokyo: Ōtsuki Shoten, 1971, p. 366.

[2] Vol. 2, no. 4.

knew what other powers the jar would bring."[1] In the language
of art criticism, the black jar symbolises female sexuality; prior to
Kōkichi, no feminist in modern Japan had invoked this
symbolism. Control of one's sexuality as one's own became an
important feminist issue in Japan only in the 1970s—sixty years
after Kōkichi had designed that cover page. Unfortunately, in the
first decades of twentieth-century Japan no-one understood
Kōkichi as a pioneer feminist. Quite the opposite: in that feudalistic society Kōkichi's independent and magnanimous personality
not only brought disaster to her but also became the principal
ingredient for attacks on the women of *Seitō*.

Around this time, Kōkichi and a few women from *Seitō* who
were interested in learning more about the conditions of working
women, visited Yoshiwara and were received by *geisha*. Yoshiwara
was the famous entertainment area formed when the licensed
quarters throughout Edo (old Tokyo) were forcibly assembled
into one area during the Edo period. Going to Yoshiwara, or
Yoshiwara *tōrō*, was synonymous with being entertained by
geisha. Geisha welcome guests by playing the *Shamisen*, dancing
Nihon buyō or singing *Nagauta*, and eating, drinking and chatting
together. Hearing that Kōkichi had not only previously done the
unladylike thing of drinking alcoholic beverages in a bar with
friends, but had also visited Yoshiwara, a newspaper reporter
scandalised the events. The press instigated what were to be
called the Yoshiwara Tōrō and Multicoloured Cocktail incidents.
Entering a bar and drinking alcohol, calling a *geisha* to your
private room—these were forms of entertainment permissible
only for men. Harsh criticism of the so-called "new women"
boiled up and threatened the lives of the women of *Seitō* as a
result of the scandal. Former *Seitō* member Ide Fumiko recalls in

[1] Vol. 2, no. 5, 1912, p. 48.

Seitō no onnatachi (The women of *Seitō*),[1] that the magazine's headquarters were bombarded with stones and a death threat made to one of the employees.

The more the newspapers fussed about "new women", the more the concept became popular. Greater numbers of like-minded women hid from their families to secretly read *Seitō* from cover to cover. However, in the midst of the journalistic frenzy, Raichō met Okumura Hiroshi, a younger man; her protective attitude toward Kōkichi suddenly altered. Raichō became obsessed with her affair with Okumura. Kōkichi, in turn, became insanely worried about the change in Raichō. After briefly publishing the magazine *Safuran* (Saffron), Kōkichi, eventually, broken-hearted over Raichō, abandoned the man's name she had adopted, threw away Japanese art and, in accordance with the stipulations of the feudal family system, wore traditional bridal wear as she wed into ceramic artist Tomimoto Kenkichi's old Nara family.

Raichō's whitewashing of homosexuality in her auto-biography *Watashi no aruita michi* (The path I've walked),[2] coupled with Kōkichi's silence upon marriage, has pressured most scholars to ignore their same-sex love. Mainstream Japanese feminism continues to ignore the political aspects of Kōkichi's existence, dismissing the love relations of her and other such women as merely childish pastimes.

The other famous literary couple are Nakajō (Miyamoto) Yuriko—famous for novels such as *Mazushiki hitobito no mure* (The throng of poor)[3]—and Russian translator Yuasa Yoshiko.

[1] Tokyo: Kaiensha Shobo, 1975.
[2] Tokyo: Nihon Tosho Sentā, 1994 [1955].
[3] Serialised in *Chūō kōron*, 1916.

They met at the house of writer Nogami Yaeko in 1924. Yuriko was twenty-five, Yoshiko twenty-seven. Yuriko was a daughter of the upper class who, upon publishing her first serial novel, *Mazushiki hitobito no mure*, at seventeen had been praised as a genius. She, however, considered herself to be stuck in a boring marriage and, despite being of a higher social class, she envied Yoshiko who lived quietly by herself and received enough money from her uncle to study Russian without taking on other employment.

About a month and a half after their first meeting, Yoshiko visited Yuriko at her mountain home where, hidden away from her husband, she was working on a new novel. Yuriko was shocked at the strength of her attraction to Yoshiko. A year later, she finally separated from her husband and began living with Yoshiko. Cohabiting with Yuriko, Yoshiko was able to devote herself entirely to her translation work. She published a translation of Chekhov's writing (*Chekhov shoseki shū*),[1] the culmination of one and a half year's work. Having gained confidence from it, she felt Russian translation was to be her life work. After three years together, Yoshiko decided to study in the Soviet Union.

Fights between the pair became frequent from the time of Yoshiko's decision to study abroad. Yuriko became the object of desire for male friends, who dismissed the couple's relationship as merely friendship; this sent Yoshiko mad with jealousy. Their personal letters also indicate that, much as the pair were in love, they avoided sexual contact. Inevitably, most of the emotional strain fell on Yoshiko. This suppressed sexual desire burst forth in violent jealousy and dangerously cornered their lives.

[1] Shinchōsha, 1928.

Yoshiko and Yuriko continued living together briefly after their return from the Soviet Union. Yuriko, however, had become a staunch believer in communism and was passionately consumed by highly fashionable revolutionary ideologies. One day, when Yoshiko travelled to Kyoto to buy Chinese herbal medicine for her, Yuriko, leaving all of her belongings behind, ran away to marry Miyamoto Kenji, later the president of the Japanese communist party.

After the Second World War, when the ban preventing communist activities was lifted, Yuriko published *Dōhyō* (Signpost),[1] and *Futatsu no niwa* (Two gardens),[2] two novels about women who awaken to communism. She rewrote these semi-autobiographical works under the supervision of her husband Kenji. In these literary works, Yuriko refers contemptuously to lesbian sex as "sewage". Yuasa Yoshiko maintained her silence and withheld public comment on Yuriko's insulting description of love between women. She did, however, throw her anger into her diary:

> As for that work *Dōhyō*, it's a downright lie. It's pure meanness to whitewash the situation. What of the manifestations of her bodily passion in the last days of my relationship with her? I will not talk of this to another. I will keep it quiet, held in my breast. One hundred years hence, however, this can be brought to light.[3]

For the remainder of her life, Yoshiko carefully preserved all Yuriko had left behind. Desk, memo, pen, letters, diary; all were kept as they were for fifty-eight years after Yuriko had left without saying goodbye.

---

[1] Serialised in *Tenbō* magazine during 1947.
[2] Serialised in *Chūō Kōron* magazine in 1947.
[3] Quoted in *Yuriko dasubidanya* (Goodbye Yuriko) Sawabe Hitomi, Tokyo: Bungei Shunjūsha, 1990.

Walking through the huge grounds in the east garden of the Yoshiya Nobuko Memorial Museum, I imagined the lives of lesbians in Japan seventy years ago. This magnificent Japanese-style garden featured an artificial miniature hill and an aesthetic dry pond. Crossing over a little bridge to the opposite side of the pond there was a small arbour. I had a bird's eye view of the garden and main house as I sat on the bench in the arbour next to JJ. Yoshiya Nobuko and Monma Chiyo had built the spectacular house and gardens with their own strength. In order to keep the life and assets they had built together as their own, Chiyo, the younger of the two, was registered as Nobuko's adopted daughter a few years before Nobuko's death. Still today, some same-sex partners in Japan, at risk of having the relationship they have developed over many years swiftly erased by their family, formally register themselves in an adoptive relationship.

After Nobuko's death, in accordance with her will, the magnificent house she had shared with Chiyo was transformed into the Yoshiya Nobuko Memorial Museum. Chiyo, now known as Yoshiya Chiyo, and several friends were appointed as the board of directors for the museum. Apparently Chiyo resided as caretaker in one of the museum rooms.

I was captured by complex thoughts as I gazed over the museum's gardens. What did Chiyo do in the time after Nobuko's death? I had no way of knowing because the museum had scratched out any trace of Chiyo, the woman who had silently supported Nobuko's prolific work from the shadows for fifty years.

"Hey, one day let's free this museum from herds of straight couples."

Leaving the Yoshiya Nobuko museum behind, JJ and I, munching on famous handmade rice crackers, started home through the crowds of straight couples on Kamakura's main street.

Chapter 10

DOCUMENTS

Be it Tokyo, Sydney, or Perth, whether on holiday or in everyday life, one never knows when an accident or hazardous situation will present itself. My mind always spun at the thought of possible problems which might interrupt our lives should either JJ or I be involved in a serious accident.

What if, for example, there is an unforeseen accident and I become unconscious? Who has the right to sign documents authorising surgery or other necessary procedures?

In a ward with a sign reading "Entrance to Immediate Family Only," who has the right to care for me?

In the worst scenario, who has the right to treasure mementoes of our precious time together?

Who has the right to authorise brain death, autopsy, organ donation?

Who has the right to attend the funeral?

To just whom do these rights extend?

JJ's family knew of and understood her relationship with me. I felt sure they would follow and respect the wishes she'd outlined in documents left with a lawyer in Perth. There was no immediate worry in that regard. I shivered, though, just thinking about how, under the Japanese system, my father and his family would act should something happen to me. Unless we made arrangements in advance, if something serious did eventuate, the personal life that JJ and I shared would crumble before the current system of legal rights. Returning to Tokyo from Australia, I knew the time had come to tackle problems we'd shelved for too long.

Since my mother's death over fifteen years before, I'd grown increasingly fearful of the attitudes my father, now in his eighties, and the family around him held. For years I'd avoided them. My fears were deeply related to the fact that my father and most of his family were doctors.

My father runs a small private hospital and is president of the local medical association in the most conservative part of Japan, rural Gifu. Since childhood, seeing my father in action on many occasions, I grew up witnessing how doctors, police, politicians and medical universities made secret dealings out of the public sphere. Many private consultations were held late at night and always ended with these men of power matching their stories in whispers. "I'll say that, so you just follow through and do it." "Don't let anyone else in on this, okay, this is just between you and me."

Important family decisions were made in the same fashion and, for my brothers and I as children, there was nothing as fearful as our father's late-night whispers. The suggestion to take me to a psychiatric hospital when I rebelled as a teenager, the meticulous plan to put sedatives in my brother's milk when he was highly strung with examination stress. "Please, don't do it." Faced with my father who soon proposed medical treatments, my mother spent whole nights trying to convince him otherwise.

The entrenched belief in secret consultations held by my father and his family of doctors is especially obvious in their thoughts towards medicines, living with illness, and death. I had a good idea how they would act if anything should happen to me.

The more serious my symptoms, the less they would tell me—let alone JJ—the truth. All life and death decisions would probably be handed down by my father and my eldest brother and, in the event of any life-threatening operations, there was also the possibility my father would sign documents to release my body for research autopsy, or organ donation. I knew this because just one year after my mother died, one of my brothers, who was also a doctor, was diagnosed with cancer. The events during his year-long fight against the disease and his death were forewarning.

I was living in Tokyo when I received a phone call from my eldest brother Yoshio, a doctor living in our family home.

"Don't be surprised by what I have to tell you. The fact is, Sachio has malignant cancer."

"What? Cancer? Why? How long have you known?"

"We found out six months ago. I thought if we told you you'd get upset and cry and then Sachio would realise that he was in a serious state. So I talked about it with the old man and we decided not to tell you."

Because I am the younger sister, because I'm not a brother, they decided I would lose all sense of reason and cause Sachio's state of health to deteriorate? I was at a loss at my eldest brother's stubborn, preconceived ideas, and the sentimental scenario he had imagined of a distraught younger sister pacified by a father and brother who harnessed control with reason.

"Six months ago? Why didn't you tell me straight away?"

"Because, as I said, it's a secret from Sachio. The cancer has spread to his spinal cord, so they can't operate. It is a very malignant form and he'll be lucky if he lives another year. If he should find out, he might attempt suicide from shock. The old man and I decided to keep it a secret because if you came and saw him and got all upset, then Sachio would find out and that would be the end. When you come, make sure you act calmly. You mustn't let him know that it's cancer, understand. Whatever you do don't let anything on while you're in the ward."

Sachio was thirty-one, married and had two small sons aged one and three. My immediate thought was that, if there was no way they could operate, if he had only one year left, then surely, for his children's sake alone, they should tell him the truth. However, it was common procedure in cancer treatment at the beginning of the 1980s for medical staff to withhold the name of the illness from the patient. Many cancer patients in Japan today are still kept from knowing the truth about their own condition.

For a while, when I went to see my brother, I couldn't tell him the truth. Then one day when I was massaging his hands and feet, he whispered in a subdued voice, "I don't want to die." As a doctor, one who was conducting cancer research for his doctoral dissertation, there was no way he could have been ignorant of his own condition. From that time on, living with illness and death became a topic of conversation between us.

One time I tried to comfort him. "It isn't just you who dies. Death comes equally to all of us, it is just a matter of whether it comes early or late." To which he stared vacantly, replying that he couldn't accept he would die so soon.

"When we were young, you were so sickly and always crying, but look at how strong you are now," he said once with a wry smile. Because of my eldest brother Yoshio's comments about my expected hysteria, I'd refused to let myself cry when in Sachio's ward, but the moment I saw that smile, uncontrollable tears flowed.

When Sachio's pain was intense in the last stages of the disease, I copied the *Prajna-paramita sutra*, a popular Buddhist scripture, and gave it to him. "I prayed that even if there is no way you can be helped, at least the pain can be taken away," I explained. Breathing with difficulty, Sachio reached out his thinning arm and, repeating the words "thank you", placed the handwritten copy in the breast pocket of his pajamas. He kept it with him until he died. I don't think it was death itself that my brother feared. I think it was most difficult for him to spend his remaining precious time experiencing unrelenting pain.

In the weeks before his death, Sachio, face full of death, pleaded, "Please, tell me the truth, help me." But my father and my eldest brother never once told him the name of his illness. Until the end they both replied with lies. "The truth? It's as I told you before. It isn't malignant. Persevere. Keep fighting."

My eldest brother and my father truly believe that to not tell the truth, to hide family pain with fake smiles and calls to "persevere", are acts of beauty. I felt fully the influence of media representations of cancer as a beautifully dramatic scenario.

As snow fell dully one cold January morning, my brother painfully took his last breaths in the university hospital. Even though Sachio was unconscious and unable to respond, I was convinced that he could hear the voices of those around him. His wife Mitchan and I sat holding his hands and talking to him. "It's okay. We're here. We're right beside you."

Suddenly a number of medical staff flew into the room and my brother was enveloped in what seemed to be major panic. "He's dead," someone said to me. "But his heart is still beating." I pointed to the electrocardiogram which showed intermittent waves of weak activity. Very quickly someone switched off the machine. "Never mind about that. All family out of the room please. Out now!" We were promptly ordered from the scene. In moments my brother's body was whisked away on a stretcher.

A little while later my father appeared from along the corridor. "I just stood in at the autopsy." I couldn't believe my ears. I was stunned—it was the first time I'd heard anything about my brother being taken to autopsy. Was it necessary to carry out one so quickly?

I was trembling. Was my brother really dead? In those last moments I'd sensed his body was preparing for death. Although he couldn't respond to us, I knew he definitely could hear our voices. When the medical staff flew into the room and we were thrown outside, my brother was only midway to death. I must have looked terribly shocked.

"He's dead. He was a doctor at this research hospital, so he had to cooperate." Mitchan whispered to me, a mere shell of her former self.

Amidst the confusion, all I understood was that my brother had been autopsied immediately upon his so-called death. The organs invaded by cancer had been removed to contribute to the cancer research he himself had been working on at the hospital. I have nothing against autopsy itself, yet I wasn't convinced of their need to cut up a body which had only just been pronounced dead. Sachio may have stopped breathing, but, even so, he was not just a corpse. Questions remain with me since experiencing my brother's death. Perhaps my doubts arose because I was the only one not informed of the autopsy before it was carried out. This could mean that even today I am misinterpreting the situation. If that is the case, I'm relieved for Sachio's sake more than anything. Since experiencing the events surrounding my brother's autopsy, I personally have grown to entertain doubts about brain death and organ donation.

This episode alone is enough to explain the anxiety I feel toward my father and his family. Our family system revolves around the following beliefs:

Never tell the truth.
All important decisions will be made in deepest secret by father
    and eldest son.
Decisions made will be delivered as orders to the rest of the family.
All efforts will be made to cooperate with autopsy and organ
    donation, for the sake of medical research and progress.

What disturbs me the most is that my father and his family
are not exceptional in their views: this is the mainstream trend
in Japanese medicine. In this society only the "immediate family"
has legal rights. What would happen to someone like me who
takes issue with procedures for establishing brain-death should I
ever have an unexpected accident and the right to decide my
own life and death is handed to my family? Reflecting on
Sachio's death, I resolved to clearly document my wishes in order
to legally protect JJ and me, and our rights.

That said, lawyers in Japan are far removed from the everyday life
of ordinary people. Unlike Australia, there are no advertisements
in gay newspapers and magazines for legal offices showing
lawyers' smiling faces. I had no idea how the issue of legal rights
of lesbian partners would be treated. Would we be thrown out of
the office? Looked at strangely? Laughed out as if we'd made a
joke? Would I have to explain "lesbian", beginning with
sexuality? And how much would the consultation and final
documentation cost? I decided to erase the clouds of doubt which
had previously floated in my mind and prevented me from taking
action.

"If it doesn't work, it doesn't work. Let's just try and see what
happens." I encouraged myself to make the relevant inquiries.

The first person I contacted was a lawyer who'd been
involved in women's issues for years, acting to protect the rights of
rape victims. Due to the effort Japanese lesbian activists made as

early as the 1970s to build a sturdy support network for women who had been raped, there were a few lawyers who, while not lesbians themselves, were not prejudiced against lesbians. This busy lawyer's time was scheduled down to a second. She did, however, make the time to talk with me. Unfortunately she was leaving to study in the United States in a month and was fully engaged with her current cases, making it impossible to take on anything new. "Do you mind if the lawyer is a man?" she asked before continuing. "The lawyer handling the Fuchū Youth House case is probably perfect for homosexual partnership rights." And so she introduced me to Nakagawa, one of the Fuchū case lawyers.

The Fuchū Youth House case was being contested by the gay and lesbian group Occur. In 1990, when Occur used the Fuchū complex for a weekend retreat, they introduced themselves as a gay group at the regulatory morning group meeting. They had then been harassed during their stay by other groups using the facilities. In the ongoing legal case, the group were fighting to revoke the ban that the Tokyo Metropolitan Government had subsequently enforced, preventing not only Occur from using those facilities again, but any gay and lesbian groups from using any municipal youth accommodation facilities in the future. Although the Tokyo Metropolitan Government had been ordered to revoke the ban and pay damages in 1994, the case was now in its second sitting due to the Government's appeal.

I decided to meet with Nakagawa straight away.

"Hmmm. I see." In a bright room of the Musashino Legal Offices, Nakagawa, in rolled-up sleeves, slurped his coffee and nodded. Nakagawa, whom I've met with many times since, whether it is a warm spring day or zero degrees outside, always approaches cases with a positive attitude and rolled-up sleeves.

At first I thought it highly improbable that a lawyer, who was both straight and a man, would take on homosexual issues without the slightest hint of prejudice, so I figured Nakagawa must be gay. He is in fact, heterosexual, married, and the father of two small children. A few months after our first meeting Nakagawa confessed he'd only become involved in the Fuchū case because one of his old law student friends was a member of Occur and one of the plaintiffs.

"This friend, who also happened to be one of the plaintiffs, came out to me and at the same time asked me to represent him. It's funny really, because when we were studying I always picked on him. He was always so gloomy and I just kind of teased him because of that. I had no idea that he was gay. When he came out to me I was really surprised." Nakagawa had obviously changed over the years since he'd experienced the Fuchū case and travelled with Occur members to different countries to research international homosexual rights. I'd been nervous about just opening my mouth to say I wanted to protect my lover's rights, and was relieved when he responded clearly and without prejudice to my queries.

"Hmm, yes, I see. This is my first such case, but I'll see what I can do. An unmarried heterosexual couple actually won in court with a joint living agreement as the basis of their case. We can use this agreement as the blueprint to draw up a same-sex joint living agreement. We can also make you a will and register both documents at the notary office. Registering them ensures the contents can be forcibly enacted should your affairs not be carried out in accordance to your wishes."

Nakagawa proceeded to explain the negative possibilities.

"However, even if we draw up these documents, as this will be the first case of its kind in Japan, there is no guarantee that the contents will be enforced under current law. The validity of a joint living agreement drawn up between a same-sex couple will, and I hate to say this, unfortunately only be tested should you die, Marou. Nonetheless, should the matter be taken to court, the very existence of the documents will form grounds for legal action. It will be an adventure, I can't promise anything more. Is that okay?"

That was more than okay. In fact, I was so surprised listening to Nakagawa, who, knowing of my relationship with JJ, was suggesting drawing up the papers and registering them, that I leant forward into the desk. "Really? Do you really think we can make these papers?" To think that here, in Japan, in my own lifetime, this could actually happen. "So … so where should we start?"

"Well, first you should make a note of anything you are concerned about and bring it along to our next meeting."

With that wonderful news I hurried home.

JJ and I discussed the issues. The documents we were about to make would cost money, yet there was no guarantee they would be validated in court. Still, we decided it was worth going through the process, even if only to clearly outline the rights people in relationships like ours should legally have. JJ was, after all, no longer in a desperate visa situation. Studying at graduate school and receiving a scholarship stipend, she now had the graduation certificate necessary for finding employment here if needed. Even if the documents we drew up weren't one hundred percent guaranteed, we could legally register our wishes. If those wishes weren't honoured, we vowed we would fight.

JJ and I wrote down the problems that might eventuate should something happen to either one of us. The right to nurse, the right to make decisions, the right to hold a funeral, the right to inherit. Nakagawa took each one of them and drafted a preliminary agreement. After several days of visits to the office and exchanging faxes, our Joint Living Agreement and my Final Will and Testament were finished. The most important clause of the Joint Living Agreement states, "The right of decision rests with each partner over and above the rights of the immediate family." Another clause nominating JJ as the chief mourner at my funeral ensured that in legal terms she would be considered in a position equal to members of my birth family. Nakagawa had proposed this clause as one which would provide the most legal clout.

Two witnesses were required to register the documents as notary deeds. Nakagawa suggested that having lawyers as witnesses might make our case stronger in a worst-case scenario and he organised for a colleague to accompany us to the local notary office. Here, in Japan, in a system of family registration based on compulsory heterosexual marriage, we witnessed the processes it takes to bring legal rights to those excluded from the system. All that remained was to actually register the documents.

We arranged to meet outside the notary offices early one day at the beginning of summer. Surprisingly, the offices were within walking distance from where JJ and I lived; in fact, we often passed them on the way to the supermarket. It was easy to miss this old building in the midst of the shopping arcades.

"So this was a notary office, huh." My nervousness was abated by the office being in such close proximity.

Soon Nakagawa arrived in trademark rolled-up sleeves and wiping his brow. We entered. The dark corridor and large central wooden staircase gave the building a retro feeling, like that of the pre-war Shōwa or Taishō eras. The four of us sat around the notary official, who was suitably coiffed with retro white hair. A copy of the document Nakagawa had printed was already in the notary's hands.

"So, shall we begin?" the notary said. His face indicated confusion as to our relationship.

A notary's job is to read aloud each clause of the document clarifying the contents. "Is this correct? Do you have any comments?" the retro notary official asked all parties involved. It was obvious that in our case he had no idea how to react to JJ. In the end he decided to emphatically ask me for confirmation.

"What is written here is definitely of your own volition, is that correct? You have not been coerced into writing this by anyone, have you? By this person sitting here, for example." He pointed to JJ.

"No. These are my wishes," I answered. With which the notary placed his face close to mine and stared into my eyes. "You haven't been told that if you don't sign this you will not be looked after in old age, or something, have you?"

"No. Not at all. These are my own wishes."

After each clause was read, the questioning was repeated. Both JJ and Nakagawa sat quietly throughout; their faces openly questioned the necessity of the repetitious confirmation.

When the process of reading had finished at last, the document was signed and sealed by all present. The notary signed and sealed it last of all.

"There, it is all done. The notary deed made here today will be kept safely by us on these premises. The deed will also be kept at the city offices for one hundred years. It will be kept in good hands, safe even from fire. Wonderful, isn't it."

Having escaped from his bragging, we breathed a collective sigh of relief on the pavement outside.

"Gee, he was rather pushy. The reading usually goes fairly quickly and then it's all over," Nakagawa said.

"I wasn't sure how I should react," JJ grimaced.

"It isn't usually like this?" I ventured.

"They don't usually check and recheck. But as there wasn't any problem with actually registering it as a notary deed, there isn't anything to worry about."

Despite the slightly unnerving experience, for the first time in Japan between a lesbian couple, JJ and I had finally made a Joint Living Agreement.

Walking with JJ and Nakagawa, I looked up at the sky above Kichijōji, the town I so loved. The sky seemed unusually blue for Tokyo, or so it seemed to me.

Chapter 11

THE PARADE

Love

"You know, the first I time I came to Ni-chōme I had real trouble trying to find it." I sipped my gin and continued with one of my favourite stories. "I rang the English-language help line, TELL,[1] and they gave me the number of Occur's gay counselling line. The gay guy I talked to there me gave me the names of three lesbian bars. Luckily Nikki had given me a copy of the Japan section of a gay travel guide. The telephone numbers were still the same. It took me all my courage to ring them and ask directions."

Marou smiled. She'd heard this story many times before, but was happily listening as I told it to a new acquaintance at Kinswomyn, a small Ni-chōme bar.

"So what happened?" Machi hadn't been coming to Ni-chōme long herself. The opening of Kinswomyn nearly a year ago had instigated an increase in the number of lesbians and women-loving-women who hung out in Ni-chōme. The tiny shot bar's prices were competitive. It didn't have a cover charge or provide overpriced snack foods, so young lesbians could afford to drop in more frequently for a drink. For me Ni-chōme had always signalled brief respite from the pressures of everyday closeted existence.

[1] Tokyo English Life Line.

"Well, I came out of the station and immediately got lost. I ended up at an intersection near Ni-chōme, but made a wrong turn and panicked. I ducked into a 24-hour deli and asked the shopkeeper which way I should go. I didn't realise that in Shinjuku there was only one meaning for Ni-chōme—and that is gay. The more I walked, the more I got lost. I rang the bar I was going to at least three times to check where they were. I sure did shock the greengrocer, too, when I asked him for directions." I was laughing. It must have been bizarre for small shop owners to encounter a huge foreign woman loudly asking for directions to Shinjuku Ni-chōme, the infamous gay area of Tokyo.

"You know, you might as well have yelled, 'Where do I find the dykes?'" Marou chuckled. We were all in high spirits. We'd been discussing the first Lesbian and Gay Parade scheduled to take place in August. I wanted to be involved, but neither Marou nor I were keen on becoming part of the organising committee. Earlier in the year we had joined a group working on plans to publish a commercial lesbian magazine. The publishers, who ran what was to become the parade headquarters, had prompted talks of making a magazine by offering to publish one. The founding members of this group had taken up the offer. However, when the publishers demanded control of content by critiquing, among other things, the magazine mock-up's so-called feminist editorial stance, the group resisted. Some interviews were already completed, but the group's plan to get a stylish and informative magazine into bookstores was frozen and eventually faded out of existence.

After walking in the Perth Pride March and running beside Dykes on Bikes at the Sydney Gay and Lesbian Mardi Gras, Marou had concrete ideas for getting an entry together for the parade—Mardi Gras style.

"If you and JJ get a group together, my friends and I would love to participate," Machi gabbled in excitement. Perhaps we could increase lesbian visibility via the parade.

A few weeks earlier at a newly opened club, Marou and I had been chatting while taking a break from dancing. A woman I vaguely knew approached us. "You know, I really think you should help her out with the parade. It's tough doing it alone with the boys." She pointed to a mutual friend, who had been part of the magazine planning meetings. The coordinating committee had already been formed and the woman she indicated was one of the few lesbians involved. Both Marou and I had been at a talk session where participants briefly bantered the concept of a parade, but we had done nothing. Further developments had filtered through to us via the community grapevine. We were in the midst of making bookings for our trip to New York. The four-yearly Gay Games were being held there to coincide with Stonewall 25, the twenty-fifth aniversary of the Stonewall Riots in Greenwich Village. We planned to be spectators for the Unity 94 Gay Games, and participate in the Stonewall 25 march through central Manhattan. I was somewhat excited by the prospect of coming home to preparations for Tokyo's first ever lesbian and gay march.

"It would be such a waste if this parade opportunity faded into a remake of a dull '70s protest." Marou turned to face me once we'd been left to our own conversation. Needless to say, lesbians had taken part in street demonstrations in Tokyo before. This year alone Marou and I had marched for International Women's Day, and participated in a march and candlelight vigil for victims of war rape crimes. These were meaningful events which attracted substantial media attention. But somehow I felt impact was lost with handheld, handwritten placards and monotone slogans chanted year after year.

"They're called *Sprechchor*, from the German," Marou said when we marched for International Women's Day. "Student demos in the '60s and '70s used the same sort of chant." She almost groaned. When I commandeered the handheld megaphone and made up some lesbian calls of my own, she whooped and loudly echoed them beside me. No matter how much the Sydney Gay and Lesbian Mardi Gras might be criticised for its commercial endeavours, in Tokyo's current commercial fever I felt sure a march grounded in political content and enhanced by performances would demand attention.

Tokyo was arching into a gay and lesbian boom. For many years, *Onna o ai suru Onnatachi no Monogatari* (The story of women who love women),[1] had been the only "lesbian" publication available over local bookstore counters. A non-fiction anthology, it contained information about lesbian community groups. In 1992, activist Kakefuda Hiroko released *Lesbian de aru to iu koto* (On being lesbian).[2] In 1993, Marou released her autobiographical non-fiction *Manaita no ue no Koi* (Love upon the chopping board)[3]. A small number of activists had also recently begun the process of publicly coming out. Marou's profile alone had increased since the publication of her book and interviews in the mainstream and alternative press.

In the 1990s, television followed the print media in increasing coverage of queer Japan. News clips snuck in alongside sensationalised tabloid talk shows which interviewed *okama* and *onabe*, transsexuals and transgender professionals who worked in the bar scene—one of the few employment areas which offered stable employment. The gay rights group Occur,

[1] Tokyo: JICC, 1987.
[2] Tokyo: Kawadeshoboshinsha.
[3] Tokyo: Takarajimasha.

who were in their second court hearing against the Tokyo Metropolitan Government, called occasional press conferences, some of which received air time. On cinema screens, gay, lesbian, bisexual and transgender images received wider exposure in Tokyo's annual gay and lesbian film festival. In the year preceding the parade, the film festival had splintered into two separate groups and Tokyo supported two festivals in the space of six months.

"We could do something like Mardi Gras. Get a group of dykes together for a dancing team." I had visions of leather and feathers, political messages jazzed up with colourful posters. Marou imagined choreographed action and powerful copy. Marou and I set about planning a dyke entry in the parade. We made contact with members of the now-defunct magazine group and tapped into the lesbian network.

Returning from New York and the Stonewall 25 celebrations, I was highly charged. After numerous telephone calls and discussions, six interested women turned up for our initial meeting in early July. Over coffee I presented an overview of our proposal. Marou talked about approaching a friend to choreograph a routine. In a matter of weeks we had formed what we would latter call *Kokusai Bian Renmei*—the International Bians United (IBU). Group consensus decided our eventual name. *Bian* was a term Tokyo lesbians used to reference themselves. It was a sort of code, one that couldn't easily be deciphered by unknowing passers-by. *Bian* was an act of reclamation, a challenge to the wider prejudiced public who, among other epithets, insisted on calling us "*lezu*". One of our slogans in the parade read "Put the *bian* back into *lezu*! LESBIAN."

Marou's friend Kawai, who'd worked with her in theatre and was later a member of a highly acclaimed dance theatre group, agreed to help us with the project. Kawai had choreographed a routine for Marou and I eight months earlier which we'd performed at the opening of our band Kinbiren's New Year gig. Now, in her spare time she choreographed a routine for ten untrained lesbian dancers. Every Friday night for the next six weeks we assembled in a carpark in Aoyama and practised for two or three hours. After rehearsals we walked down to the closest donut store to discuss costumes, music and van decorations. Two members of IBU were also part of the organising committee for the parade. They shared committee information, and we talked about strategies, media dealings and possible routes. On weekends we gathered at the local women's centre. Here we rehashed our dance steps and consulted about costume materials, posters and hundreds of details.

As a group we were varied in skills, time availability, ideas, flexibility, energy and flair. My personal vision was of Mardi Gras; it was one that Marou shared. I had ideas and willingness to work. Marou had both those, and experience in set design, set construction and multi-party theatre collaborations. The ideas that I could only verbalise or badly sketch, she could translate into creation. During six weeks, our room in Kichijōji south became cluttered with notebooks, CDs, rehearsal tapes, off-cuts of material and flagpoles for the rainbow flags. Our words bounced off the walls as we discussed parade particulars night after night.

"I'll ring Marou-tachi [Marou's] and let you know if I find any good music." Marou's? I automatically grimaced the moment anyone used those words. Despite our collaborative efforts, I noticed a tendency to refer to Marou and myself as a set; as "Marou-tachi". Sure, *tachi* made the phrase plural, but I still felt sucked into some kind of blanketing "we".

"It's Marou and Claire." It became my catch phrase.

"Perhaps we can go to Marou-tachi's apartment."

"Marou and Claire's apartment." I felt my personal efforts were being blended into Marou's. Around this time I also began to feel an increasing gap between the persona JJ, and myself, Claire. In the pages of Marou's original book, I had hidden behind the name JJ. I hadn't felt able to allow myself to be identified. Marou and I had discussed possible name alternatives. Betty didn't suit me, neither did Andrea, or Jennifer. To Marou, I was nothing but Claire. I agreed, but the fear of being recognised as Claire by people as obscure as university professors, immigration officials, and the karate specialist next door was suffocating. We had finally decided to use the pseudonym JJ—the name of a stuffed toy bear that I'd given Marou. JJ and Claire—the gap was becoming painfully noticeable to me, but I clung onto JJ until well after the first lesbian and gay parade.

Ostensibly our group shared tasks. Eventually, however, work filtered to people who had either the skills or the sheer determination necessary to pull the job off. We broke off into groups: artistic direction, placard design, slogan creation, costume design, music selection, van decorations, organising committee go-between, driving and delivery. On top of those responsibilities, we all tried to dance as best we could. Although each member worked hard to get her body around the dance steps, none of us were professionals. Our choreographer didn't let us off with that excuse. "If you are dancing in front of people, you must dance at as high a level of presentation as possible." Kawai spent hours standing in the rain drumming the steps into our feet. The least we could do was practise by ourselves whenever possible.

Through a contact in the women's rights movement, we borrowed a van. It was one used in political campaigns: the type which cruised streets in the weeks leading up to local elections, broadcasting the promises of candidates riding inside. It had a microphone linked to a loudspeaker on the roof. The roof also supported a platform where candidates could stand and give speeches. The van decoration group, of which I was one, took measurements and designed ways to cover up the women's group's logo peeling from the heat. On the day of the parade, balloons and calligraphy transformed the van into an IBU art piece. Mayuki, a calligraphy major still at university, wrote our group name and slogans in black ink. With advice from one of our artist members, Kazuko, we painted the Japanese fans used in our dance routine shocking pink. The pink contrasted with our costumes. Our concept was simple and black—the more skin exposed the better. Black curved plastic extensions jutted out from our shoulders. In a last-minute rush Kazuko ordered rainbow flags through a friend in the United States. The rainbow arch we made appeared even more colourful against our black outfits. Marou, once again using theatre connections, had rented two enormous flag harnesses. Two women holding giant harnessed rainbow flags headed our dance formation.

On the day of the parade I wore dark sunglasses and a leather hat embossed with a love heart. I was out, I was proud but, like my name, I didn't want my face too exposed. Most of IBU felt the same. It was with a combination of burning pride and paradoxical fear that we assembled at eight-thirty in the morning of 28 August at the bottom of Shinjuku Chūō Park.

A crowd of about thirty people were gathered in front of the waterfall opposite the Tokyo Municipal Offices. Our starting point was the edge of Shinjuku's hotel-intense area. The parade would march past the Tokyo government buildings, continue on to pass by the south exit of Shinjuku station, turn into Meiji Dōri, cut directly through the major shopping area of Harajuku, and finish up at Miyashita Park in Shibuya. A group of us had walked the route in preparation the week before. Our dancing was timed to coincide with busy intersections. We planned to flash colourful lesbian cards at the crowd waiting at the lights of Shinjuku station and wave rainbow flags to window shoppers. Nagae, in charge of coordinating liquid refreshments and general organisation, would indicate to the sound operator when to change our marching music for our dance music. The change was the cue to form our lines and dance.

Police restrictions limited the number of vehicles permitted to participate in a demonstration. Our main IBU-member-cum-parade-organiser made arrangements to allow our van to drive at the rear of the parade. The police had blocked off one lane of traffic. We would be close to the sidewalk and in the face of shoppers enjoying the Sunday morning heat. IBU commenced the parade with a flurry of music and a swish of fans. Or so I hoped. The music system gurgled and then spluttered a strange sound. After weeks of meetings, hours spent selecting music, thousands of heated discussions and continuous rehearsals, I was a highly strung and monstrous wreck. We had planned the music to the minute. We would start out with "Go West", then go into our first dance formation. This made sure we performed right in front of the media cameras at the beginning of the parade.

"What are you doing. Put it on. Not that one. The 'Go West' tape." Never one to be kind and gentle in moments of panic, I shouted as I climbed into the IBU van. As fate would have it, I commenced the First Tokyo Lesbian and Gay Parade with my bum sticking out of a moving vehicle, shouting.

By the time we reached Miyashita Park our van, which was meant to signal the end of the parade, was somewhere near the middle. Groups of lesbians who had started walking beside the parade were now walking as part of it. A stylish group of women, dressed in cyberpunk white, imitated IBU's dance steps behind us. Marou and my friends shouted cries of encouragement as they marched behind us in a display of support for lesbian rights. A group of gay men danced alongside. A convertible draped with drag queens darted around us. We were the only group performing, and the only group with music. Everybody loved it. Our costumes and music livened the parade and were a large contributor to its overall success. Spelling out L E S B I A N on top of the Miyashita Park overwalk, doing our final "Ooooooohhhhhhh Lesbian" call as we entered the park itself, I felt an amazing natural high. Still huddled behind my sunglasses and reluctant to take off my hat, I finished the parade worrying about supplying *onigiri* to the women who had continuously danced for nearly all of the five-kilometre parade route. With an equally exhausted Nagae I dashed to buy yet another five bottles of cold drinks. Guzzling water in the shade of the only tree, I tried to put the pressure of returning the van out of mind. Chū, who had done much carting of luggage in the weeks leading up to this event, said she would return it with us later in the day.

The parade culminated in a rally where the organisers read a list of claims for lesbian and gay rights. It was greeted with cheers from the crowd, and followed by introductions of the participants. The MC was the outrageously lovable Emi Eleona—an energetic performer and musician talented at rousing any crowd. Somewhere along the line Marou and I were coaxed onto the stage. The "Go West" music started playing, and we performed the dance Kawai had choreographed for our last Kinbiren gig. Marou, dressed in rubber and vinyl, was dangerously close to dehydration and sunstroke. Calling the steps out to guide her through the performance, we finished elated, but utterly exhausted. Unable to stand much longer, we sat once again in the shade of the tree. In an attempt to relax, I focused on

Chū's lyrics. She was on the makeshift stage performing some of her best lesbian songs.

"It was a total group effort, but you know, without your skill for organisation, your motivation and sheer determination, IBU would never had made it here," I whispered to Marou and kissed her ear. We were aching all over, and only after snoozing for a couple of hours were we able to drag ourselves off to the post-parade party and celebrate with the the rest of the group.

Scenes from the parade were broadcast on the evening news. The turnout had exceeded the organisers' expectations. Over a thousand people had marched that day: an astronomical number for the first such event in Tokyo's highly conservative social climate. The words "lesbian", "gay", "drag queen" temporarily exploded onto the airwaves via sound bites given over to inter-views of our friends. Unfortunately these positive statements of sexual pride were prefaced by the newscaster's references to "homos", interspersed with interviews with passers-by who ex-pressed surprise that "they"—meaning us marchers—"really are different to us"—meaning those looking on. Some segments broadcast on the week's midday tabloid shows were footnoted by commentators bewildered by things like cross-dressing, red T-back pants and "the mysterious group of black-clothed lesbos". There was almost an element of surprise when these same commentators noticed "normally dressed people" who had proudly marched carrying placards displaying political messages.

Bian sensibilities offended, at the next IBU meeting we instigated a letter-writing campaign. Cutting and copying the relevant newspaper articles, we underlined offensive phrases, corrected misinformation, gave hints for better future coverage. Copying the Japanese school grading system, we gave grades from one, for excellence, to five, in definite need of improvement. Very few articles got high marks for non-biased reporting and positive image representation. The majority were in need of much improvement.

IBU's "Media Watch" developed out of this post-parade media dissection. I wrote up a "Media Watch" call for action and drafted copies of letters which could be sent to television stations, magazines or newspapers. We set up a telephone tree which, with one phone call, could quickly pass information on media representation from one interested party to another. If, for example, a talk-show host started talking about how disgusting woman-to-woman sex was, we could get up to twenty calls to the relevant television station within a few minutes. Our aim was for great numbers. Sometimes the volume of our calls was amplified in the constant engaged tone of the television's public relations department. Once, in a live TV show, I noticed a reference to female-to-female love relationships was reworded after a commercial break filled with telephone calls.

A number of projects spiralled independently of our loosely formed group. Mayuki and Nagae formed a video production group, Montage M, and began shooting their first video. It was a coming-out love story which they shot on a university campus, in an apartment, and on location at parade headquarters. Although individuals worked on different projects, we pooled resources. In December, Chū suggested reclaiming the Christmas Eve streets. The Lesbian Eve Kiss Performance was a project to increase lesbian visibility. We would stage a series of kiss performances on crowded Christmas Eve.

In Japan, New Year's Eve is the time for family reunion and feasting at home. Christmas is party time. The party mood is brought to climax in the weeks leading up to Eve, the

24 December. Decorations appear in shop windows, Christmas songs replace muzak, and an elaborate array of marketing campaigns begin. For couples, Eve is marketed as either a romantic evening to be spent in an expensive hotel, or a raunchy night for enjoying sexy underwear in a quirky love hotel. In this mainstream interpretation, of course, "couples" refers strictly to male and female duos. Same-sex images are invoked predominantly in the alternative couple-less version of Eve. Couple-less Eve is a time for simple parties at home, for eating cream cakes with friends. On Christmas Eve, nearly twenty women in our Lesbian Eve Kiss Performance group, dressed in variously outrageous, Christmassy or just plain silly costumes, walked from Shibuya to Harajuku. We sang dyke carols and distributed pamphlets. We kissed and appealed for same-sex love rights. In Omote Sandō, the famous boulevard in Aoyama, we performed to crowds packing the sidewalks to enjoy the trees ablaze with strings of illumination, which lined both sides of the street.

"Joy to the world, we dykes have come, to kiss on Christmas Eve." Accompanied by Chū on guitar, we belted out the altered lyrics that I wrote and Kayo translated. Euphoric at leaving a small mark on the Christmas Eve antics, we piled onto the crowded Yamanote line and took the train to Shinjuku. We sang at the central intersection in Ni-chōme, and serenaded the owners of popular lesbian bars. Later I heard a critique of our performance as being uncritically Christian-oriented, of participating in rampant commercialism. I understood the concerns, but my own private joy at kissing in a group of lesbians in the middle of Tokyo overtook the other issues. For me, and perhaps for other members of IBU at the time, this was another way to make an in-your-face challenge, to appeal for lesbian visibility by actually being visible. Many of us could not call out our own

names, but we were having deliciously outrageous fun in presenting our faces.

For pride week in June the next year, the ever energetic Chū
was a key figure with Kayo in coordinating a week of events in a
small Roppongi club. There were talk shows, an art exhibition
and a club performance party. The week culminated in an outing
at Inokashira Park in Kichijōji and a night show of lesbian and
gay videos. More than twenty dykes gathered at the park for our
outing. We displayed rainbow flags on the bows of the rowboats
we rented, and made circles of the small inner lake. Mid-week
Marou and I did our own talk show titled "An Evening in Marou
and Claire's Kitsch Room". Somewhere after officially passing
the entrance exams into my university's postgraduate programme, I shed a little more of my JJ encasing. On the set of our
kitsch room, Marou and Claire worked as a team.

In August, IBU regrouped and performed at the second
Tokyo Lesbian and Gay Parade. Our theme was "Superdyke".
This year we decorated the van with cartoon superdyke images
that Kazuko had designed, and carried colourful placards that the
group had feverishly made to complement these. Once again our
performance was the result of six weeks of rehearsal and hours of
meetings. We flew through our routines in blue capes, and
grooved to the summery melody of "Seaside Bound". Yet, in the
weeks leading up to the final parade date, I felt group politics
peak. With something like a sixth sense I smelt the beginnings
of faction fighting. Divisions had already surfaced within the
community which juggled the fine line of identity politics and
individual enjoyment. These past two years since returning from
Perth signalled my initiation into the politics of community. The
events that we had collaborated on as a group had definitely
made an impact and temporarily increased lesbian visibility.

However, unfortunately, nothing is straightforward in groups formed around shifting concepts of togetherness, or communities forced to live a delicate balance between the gaps of the so-called mainstream. I gradually felt a need to focus on myself. By the end of the parade, I wasn't just exhausted: I was bordering on burnout.

Chapter 12

COMING HOME

The AIDS Poster Project in Kyoto asked if I'd make a contribution to their upcoming exhibition. Based in Kyoto's Artscape, the AIDS Poster Project is an eclectic group of artists. The key members are affiliated with the performance group Dumb Type who had recently toured Europe with their provocative stage performance *S/N*.

The mass media was at this time in the middle of a "gay boom". Dramas featuring man-to-man or woman-to-woman romance and/or bed scenes were announced for television, and commercials also hinted gay images. The TV drama *Dōsōkai* (Class reunion) is typical of the dramas produced at the time. Despite a homophobic script, it developed myth-like status because of its trendy male actors who kissed in mediocre sex scenes. It was rumoured that the streets of Shinjuku Ni-chōme were quiet during the programme's weekly screening.

Pseudo-lesbian relationships also became fashionable advertising backdrops. One commercial for bottled water opened with a shot of a young woman, obviously home in her country town for the summer holidays, dangling her feet into a clear stream. A young woman teacher gazes gently at her from a rock close by. "Have you ever kissed?" The teacher gasps in response. Gazing into each other's eyes, their faces draw near … And then cut. A bottle of water closes the ad. The "gay boom" was founded on voyeurism, and the mass media searched furiously for any available homo/lez copy.

I hoped to launch the original Japanese version of *Love Upon the Chopping Board* at a Tokyo club. Mona Lisa, the popular night held at Tokyo's current hottest club, Gold, was where the book was launched. This club was also targeted by the media in the midst of the "gay boom". We scheduled a late-night fashion contest to commence immediately following the official book launch. The theme was "Express yourself." Sequins, feathers, rubber, vinyl, leather, tattoos, body piercing, pastel wigs; women in a range of dress delivered their fashion messages on stage while Claire and I and a few other guests awarded contest points. A magazine journalist invaded the event; she approached some women who were dancing, and asked them outrageous questions. Sensing something odd, these women grilled the reporter in return and, cover exposed, she fled the scene in a hurry. A few weeks later an article which could only have been about the book launch at Mona Lisa, titled "Tokyo: An account of infiltrating a women's only club", appeared in a weekly magazine. The article was an unsuccessful fabrication. The only thing the spying reporter exposed were her vacuous efforts to make a highly erotic evening out of the club's event-filled night, where lesbian, gay, heterosexual, bisexual and non-sexual women enjoyed themselves together.

"Unbelievable, hey." Claire laughed when I relayed the contents of the article to her. I thought it all too stupid to be angry.

The Tokyo community supported a range of events. At the height of the media's "gay boom", event coordinators took whatever advantage they could of the mass media's voyeurism. The Tokyo Gay and Lesbian Film Festival, the First Tokyo Lesbian and Gay Parade, the publication of *Phryne*, the first commercial lesbian magazine (which soon folded and was later published briefly as *Anisu*), all received a little more coverage. One, and then two years blurred past as Claire and I participated in and spoke at a variety of community events.

The AIDS Poster Project exhibition drew closer against this backdrop of events.

Luckily at this time I had ideal material for a new piece of work. An officially registered Joint Living Agreement—nothing could be more eloquent. I thought the exhibition provided a perfect opportunity to illustrate a way of legally protecting partnership rights in Japan. Even so, it was useless just exhibiting one sheet of paper. Claire and I came up with the idea of making a short video about partnership rights. The images for the video *Coming Home* were fish, *Hanafuda* cards and a hot bath.

Hanafuda cards are often used in the gambling scenes of Tōei studio's gangster movies and other Japanese films. There is nothing more striking than a gangster woman playing a hand of cards in casual kimono cast off at her shoulder to reveal the blood-red peonies tattooed there. The image of a woman gambler was perfect. We would print messages about rights on the *Hanafuda* cards, and Claire and I would play a hand while discussing the Joint Living Agreement. We decided to ask the director of *Fresh Kill*, Shu Lea Cheang, to film and edit for us. *Fresh Kill*, filmed in 1994, incorporates the story of a lesbian couple and environmental pollution, multinational corporations, race, ethnicity and the media against the backdrop of New York's Staten Island. It is an ecocybernoia film which engages interweaving contemporary issues. The film leaped across community boundaries and was praised by film lovers and critics for its cinematographic beauty, editorial speed and rhythm, and cutting-edge statements.

Claire and I met Shu Lea at a Ni-chōme club just before the AIDS Poster Project proposal was made. Director Rose Troche and the main actress from *Go Fish* also happened to be visiting the club promoting their film the same night. A girl-meets-girl story, *Go Fish* received a Teddy Bear Show at the 1994 Berlin International Film Festival. It was currently a hot topic within the community. The dance floor was transformed into a congregation place for groupies and the club was consumed by their nervous excitement. In the middle of all of this, Shu Lea, a bottle of red wine in one hand, strolled past us in front of the drinks bar. A friend introduced us.

"You are Shu Lea Cheang, director of *Fresh Kill*? Really?"

"Ah-hah." Shu Lea was currently in Tokyo promoting her film and other work. I thought it a great opportunity to ask about one small scene in the film which had me enthralled. "The Staten Island scene. Ummm. I was really interested …"

"Ah-ha."

"Especially in the scene where a cat dressed in knitwear is pushed by in a pram."

"Ah-ha." As if remembering the filming of that particular scene, Shu Lea's eyes opened wide and the red wine she was drinking spurted from her mouth. A small spot of wine landed on my white trousers.

Dodging the red wine shower I continued to ask, "Why? Why did you decide to dress the cat in knitwear?" Shu Lea's whole body shook left to right and, hitting me on the shoulder, she tried to control the onset of laughter.

Shu Lea, Claire and I established a harmonious relationship. The secret to our successful collaboration was Claire's hard work. She laboured as translator between Shu Lea, who suddenly jumps image mid-conversation, and myself, who tends to be extremely impatient. The three of us held repeated dinner meetings, made full use of our physical strength and pooled our respective connections.

The *Hanafuda* cards we created resulted from collaborative, connected efforts. *Hanafuda*, an old Japanese card game, incorporates images of nature and the four seasons with scenes from everyday life. Some of the cards feature illustrations of birds, flowers, animals, people, the moon, rain and cherry blossom viewing, and others feature calligraphy. Our idea was to transpose dyke images and messages onto the traditional cards. First, Claire and I collected queer images to substitute for nature motifs. Then Shu Lea, using her contacts with a computer graphic firm, printed them anew. Claire and I hand-pasted the composite images Shu Lea had created onto a pack of *Hanafuda*. For the cherry blossom motif we substituted a colourful rainbow backdrop. In the full moon card we placed a lesbian symbol. Instead of a sombre-looking monk, we imposed a spiky-haired dyke. In a few weeks, with a combination of cutting-edge technology and primitive pasting, we had the first set of *(les)Bian Hanafuda*.

Besides the *Hanafuda* gambling scene, we filmed everyday images of Claire and I in our tiny bath, me slicing a mackerel on the chopping board in our small kitchen, and even captured Nyan Nyan relaxing at home. Shu Lea okayed the mackerel scene in just one or two takes. Fish often appear in Shu Lea's work, and apparently eventually end up in everyone's stomachs. With Shu Lea's culinary skills, the mackerel became our main dish at dinner after filming.

We edited a children's chorus into the bath scene and children singing "As for the sparrow's teacher, *Chiichii pappa, chiipappa*" accompany the image of Claire and I trying desperately to fit into our cramped bath. The resulting comical touch is effective. *Coming Home* includes comic footage unmodified for pubic hair.

Meanwhile, one of the AIDS Poster Project's staff was a law graduate and arranged to interview a renowned legal scholar from a famous local university on the legal validity of same-sex partners' rights. With consent, a recording of the interview was made.

"That is impossible. Unthinkable. There is no way that could be done. What are you thinking? Absolutely impossible." The legal expert's assertions of disbelief jarred when we played the tape back. For the final exhibition piece, we placed the Joint Living Agreement and our video footage beside a tape of the legal expert screaming "Absolutely impossible!" A fitting juxtaposition. A re-edited version of the short video entitled *Coming Home* has since played at gay and lesbian film festivals overseas.

As a result of this video collaboration, I also appear briefly in Shu Lea's collaborative video work *fingers and kisses* which was filmed within the Japanese lesbian community during the same year. I appear among the opening titles in mirrored sunglasses, on a white feather stool, wearing a vinyl jacket and fluttering my white gloved hands in front of the camera.

Shooting that scene was downright scary. After searching inner-city Tokyo for the perfect location, Shu Lea and I ended up in a side street near Kichijōji station. We decided to film on the staircase leading up to a "date-club". The mirrored staircase reflected the neons perfectly. As Shu Lea was filming me moving my hands towards the camera, I heard a low voice from behind me.

"Hey. You two. What are you doing here?"

As I fluttered my hands at the camera I glanced over in the direction of the voice. Two *yakuza* men dressed in black suits were glaring at us from the top of the stairs. Paying no attention to them, Shu Lea motioned me to keep moving my hands, which had temporarily ceased fluttering.

"It's okay. Okay." With no concern for the men on the stairs, Shu Lea continued filming.

"We are just filming my hands. We'll be finished in a minute." Having no choice but to keep moving my fingers, I nervously explained our behaviour.

"What? Filming? What do you mean, filming? Film the club's sign and we won't let you off lightly." One of the men came done the stairs and gruffly whispered a threat in my ears.

"Yes, I understand. Just the hands. We definitely will not film the signs." I replied brightly, and they disappeared.

"See, I told you it was alright."

Why is that Claire is never here at times like this?

Ten minutes later the gravelly voice was right behind my head. Looking behind I saw that two of them were now sandwiching me.

"Hey, I told you to stop. Why won't you listen?"

"Okay. Finished." Shu Lea switched off the camera and began to move away.

As a consequence of this image of activism, Claire and I began to stand out at clubs, at bars and on panel discussion. *Coming Home* and *fingers and kisses* were released in Japan as part of a collection of Shu Lea's collaborative works filmed both here and in America, also entitled *fingers and kisses*. Following the AIDS Poster Project exhibition, Claire and I have also taken more part in panel discussions focusing on the issue of homosexuality and legal rights.

"I'd really like to have a relationship like yours." With increasing frequency young women approached us to talk about our relationship and the documents we had registered. We have also received inquiries about the Joint Living Agreement from couples in long-term relationships.

The price for standing out, however, is that Claire and I are easily remembered, and easily caricatured. We were cameoed cartoon-like in an issue of the lesbian magazine *Anisu* published during the "gay boom". Despite the obvious exaggeration, I sensed a kind of warmth and friendship in the caricature and enjoyed reading the cartoon. In all honesty, though, I am distressed when images of Claire and I transpose into writings critical of our private life. My published work has included pieces on Nyan Nyan, so I felt stabbed in the throat upon reading a passage about a nameless lesbian couple who enjoyed clubbing and owned a cat. The passage criticised the documents that this couple drew up as equivalent to heterosexual marriage.

Some people seriously responded to the issue of same-sex legal rights which Claire and I focused on in our notary deeds, exhibition and video work. Some others interpreted our activities simply as a misguided example of same-sex marriage. Neither Claire nor I are easily tricked into illusions of everlasting love predestined to continue until death. That is why a clause in our Joint Living Agreement states that either of us can end the agreement in the presence of a witness.

"Our agreement directly addresses the legal standing of relationships other than marriage. It is one method of protecting partner's rights from the patriarchical *koseki* (family register) system. The mutual trust of the parties involved forms the basis of the agreement itself. The content of that trust depends on the parties involved. I believe that many people, regardless of sexuality, should draw up similar agreements and subvert the marriage and *koseki* systems which give rights to limited groups in society." No matter how many times I explained the reasons behind our registered agreement, to sour feminists the image of Claire and I enjoying ourselves clubbing, or participating in queer activist events, seemed to be nothing more than a living example of two people caught in illusory matrimony.

A critique which equates demands for same-sex partners' rights with heterosexist marriage might have been a useful strategy many years ago if used against heterosexist couples in positions of power. Unfortunately, however, heterosexist couples, drunk on the fantasy of romantic love, are seldom dragged into the debate. If lesbian couples are forever expected to be the embodiment of an ideal feminist society, Japanese feminism's idealist theories and the practice of lesbians are destined to tangle and become distorted.

Excluding an almost ten-year break in the 1980s when I was involved in theatre, twenty years have passed since I first learnt of the Japanese lesbian and gay community. I find myself asking, have there truly been no concrete advancements in achieving rights for queer people during those twenty years?

"South Africa's new constitution includes a sexuality rights clause."

"They say that same-sex marriage has been recognised in Denmark."

"It seems the state of Hawaii will approve the same-sex marriage bill."

"Some North American companies give partnership benefits to same-sex partners."

Even today in Japan, when news of rights gained by homosexuals overseas is made known, people collectively sigh and make plans to migrate to countries with greater legal rights.

It was the same in the 1970s. News about gains in homosexual rights overseas arrived and people sighed. Sadly, time is all that passes by as people are carried away by media-induced gay booms and idealistic utopian discourses.

Being a homosexual does not entail being someone's ideal. It is not an occupation. It isn't a form of self-realisation; for me, it isn't even wholly representative of my personal identity. It is an issue which clearly exposes where power lies and where it does not. It is an issue of power permanently attached to my life and in need of immediate resolution.

The end of the mass media's speedy "gay boom" cycle is already in sight. It changes from "gay" to "drag queen", from "drag queen" to "sex-changes", from "sex-changes" to "environmental hormones" at an urgent pace.

Chapter 13

恋 **DAYS SPENT WITH NYAN NYAN**

I met Nyan Nyan sixteen years before I met Claire.

At the time I was living in a dilapidated wooded framed house in Kōenji. Each town situated along the Chūō line is said to have its own particular atmosphere. Shinjuku is the enormous play spot which includes Ni-chōme, home to hundreds of gay bars. In the 1970s, Kokubunji was the town to which folksingers and hippies drifted. Kōenji was where unknown rock singers congregated. I didn't mind where I lived, as long as it was in Tokyo, had a good transport system, was close to the station and local public bath. In an attempt to get my life back in order a year after the elopement incident, I vacated my Shinjuku apartment, found a new job and moved to Kōenji.

Before Kōenji was redeveloped, the town was a crisscross of lanes too narrow for cars to pass through. It was a haven for feral cats. Owning pets was a major trend at the time. Long-haired cats with blue eyes were all the rage, but there was still no end to the number of cats abandoned. Because of the relative safety of Kōenji, cats there had developed into a unique breed through intergenerational crossbreeding. The majority were white short-haired tabbies, or tortoiseshell Japanese *mike*, resembling cats that were common in my childhood, but which had become rare by the 1970s. Although cynical about the current trend to breed new and commercialised breeds, I was fond of the cats in the area and referred to them as the "pure Japanese Kōenji Breed".

Old half-broken handrails, which could be used for *hanami* in the spring, surrounded the outside of the old house where I lived in Kōenji. One large cherry tree stood in the garden.

It was late one spring night.

I could hear the ceaseless cries of a cat. Unable to sleep, I reluctantly got up, opened the window and looked outside. The cries came from the top of the cherry tree in the garden. Still in my pyjamas, I went out to the bottom of the cherry tree and stared up. A kitten was stuck on the edge of one of the branches. Unable to get down, it was in a severe panic. I climbed onto the concrete fence to assess the situation. The branch was so high up that, even from the top of the fence, I couldn't reach it. If I stood on my toes and stretched up to the sky as far as I could, I was still about one metre away from the kitten. After I had tried for about thirty minutes it was clear there was nothing to do but have the kitten jump into my arms.

"It's alright. I promise I'll catch. Jump!" I called out to the kitten a number of times. It was easy to tell the kitten to leap from such height, but if I couldn't catch it, it would fall ten metres from the tree and smash into the ground. As though relieved at being found by someone, the kitten had calmed a little, but still seemed hesitant to jump. I wasn't a hundred percent sure if we would achieve success. There was no other way.

The kitten sighed.

I stretched out both arms and, so as not to frighten it, quietly repeated my calls. "It's okay. See. I promise I'll catch you."

The eyes of the bewildered kitten looked directly into the depths of mine. Those were intelligent-looking eyes. Nodding as if in realisation, in a flash the kitten made a huge jump toward my arms.

In the next sixteen years before I met Claire, Nyan Nyan, the kitten who had been stuck in the cherry tree, and I experienced a lot together. A couple of years after she came down from the tree, Nyan Nyan had a litter of kittens. Unable to care for any more, I searched for adoptive parents. The flyers I posted at a specialist cat pet shop attracted attention, and Nyan Nyan was scouted by a cat photographer. She briefly became a Japanese tortoiseshell cat model. We were both getting busier. In addition to my daytime work, my contact with activists increased. Nyan Nyan followed me halfway down our street in the mornings, and came to welcome me home at night. Days continued of catching the rush-hour commuter train to the office, working until five, spending time in heated discussion with various people at meetings and newsletter editorial gatherings, and returning home late at night to Nyan Nyan. I worked until late on the article I was writing for the second edition of *Za Daiku* (The dyke) about the romance between Hiratsuka Raichō and Otake Kōkichi. Most weekends were spent preparing for, or giving, parties at home. I met many new people in these busy days.

I gradually regained my energy. But, at the same I had a strange feeling that I was growing further away from important things. Experiencing life's uplifts, excitement, finding beauty, discovering or creating a moment of comfort: leading a life with a schedule planner full of gatherings, and actually doing what you want to do are two different things. I was fundamentally moved when I came across the as yet unknown theatre group Aoitori (Bluebird) who had recently appeared within the world of theatre. Aoitori's performances were like no other I had experienced. No matter how radical or shocking 1970s underground theatre had been, it told men's stories and was often sentimental. Aoitori's stage performances expressed the very things I was searching for, but the initial impact was too great for me to realise that. I became confused about what it was I really wanted to do. I was so racked by indecisiveness I paid 5000 yen an hour for counselling to a counsellor who had just returned from studying in America. I single-mindedly threw all of my energy into explaining my confusion to her. While doing so, my own situation—the fact that I was putting off what I really wanted to do and was defending my actions while talking to this counsellor, but unable to stop myself doing so—suddenly appeared ridiculous. I decided to listen my own voice which was telling me to stop—stop talking and make a decision.

After one hour of counselling, I paid the account and said, "Thanks for listening. I know what I should do now." I went to leave. Looking shocked the counsellor stopped me.

"Huh? Hang on a minute. What do you mean you know? Let's have you come back a few more times so we can analyse your issues."

"No thanks. I've had enough."

I became focused on making stage performances with Aoitori. Two months before a new season was scheduled, we would return from intensive workshopping retreats in the country and begin rehearsals. New scenes appeared one after the other, based on études the group improvised. Each new scene prompted another series of requests for nearly impossible stage sets or props. The artistic team, which included only myself and two or three others, literally sweated. The words "that is impossible" were forbidden; we had to make the necessary sets and props before the production began.

Set construction was arduous, and the artistic team did have some challengingly enjoyable moments. Making the set for the production *Aru hi sesse to* (Diligently one day) which was performed at the small theatre Tiny Alice, was particularly enjoyable. The main scene of the story was a storeroom, in the middle of which we placed a large wardrobe with automatic doors which would allow a myriad of props and people to enter and exit. The stone wall set behind the storeroom was designed to suddenly crumble loudly in the middle of the play, only to reappear in perfect condition a few minutes later. As all the group's pooled finances were spent maintaining our rehearsal space, there was no workshop for set construction. Miyamoto, a fellow artistic team member, and I spent a week commuting to a friend's ceramic art studio. We reclaimed a wardrobe which had been thrown out as trash, and designed a door which would open and close in time with the subtle actions on stage. We also began the detailed work which would enable the contents of the wardrobe to change within the short minutes of each scene. With the helpful advice of the ceramic artist on how to make the crumbling wall appear realistic, we mixed chamotte, an expensive ceramic art material, with gypsum and experimented with colour and the crumbling effect. We carted the sample we'd made to rehearsals so that the performers could test the effect of their baseball bat prop on the fence. We devoted our time to creative inventions. We also spent time snoozing and chatting, warming our legs under the table heater on the second floor of the studio while waiting for the gypsum to dry in the cold winter sun. It was a harmonious time of congenial hard work.

During this period, new work fountained creatively. *Natsu no omoide* (Memories of summer) and *Cinderella*, representative works which supported the continuation of the company, were both created at this time. The wall of the apartment in *Cinderella*, first performed at the Suzunari theatre in Shimokitazawa, was made from a panel which opened, closed, moved and then totally disappeared. We made it on the road in front of our rehearsal space in a remote suburb of Tokyo. *Natsu no omoide*, the play for which Aoitori became well known, was also first performed at the Suzunari. It required a cloth forest gradually extending from the back of the stage to the far end of the audience, which we made in a large lecture room we rented at the Kichijōji Community Centre. The artistic team lugged several sewing machines in and mobilised our friends to sew the cloth. The equipment which exploded in the laboratory scene was adapted from instruments secretly borrowed from the University of Tokyo's physics department. We purchased performance explosives from a specialist shop and used detonating apparatus. I made a mistake once when I was setting up the detonators and burnt my eyebrows and eyelashes. Injuries were commonplace for the artistic team.

These works were also performed outside Tokyo. In due time in the 1980s, the scripts became regulars at national high school theatre festivals. This unknown theatre group quickly became popular in the space of a few years. During that time I became totally absorbed in this work. I loved each beautifully amusing scene and felt sure I would remember each one. However, there are things called "best seasons" in cultural activities, and, this formative period was in fact the best for both those involved in creating, and those in the audience.

Aoitori along with Gekidan Sanjūmaru (300 Theatre Company) and Noise were new wave theatre companies which emerged out of underground theatre groups of the 1970s. Although the mass media extolled the early 1980s as the "women's era", life for women was anything but easy. It was one thing if you were performing traditional *Kabuki* and receiving funding from the government's Culture Agency, but in the world of theatre, even the men were badly off. If the performers were going to make a living from acting, it was necessary to strengthen the name value and reputation of the company, and to increase audience numbers. To suit larger theatre spaces with capacity to seat bigger numbers, our stage installations also needed to increase in size. The method of spending months working laboriously to fulfil detailed set requirements initially adhered to in the company's formative years was abandoned. Due to the fire prevention regulations of the large theatre spaces, it was considered safer to order work from commercial workshops. Money was invested in advertising and posters, and salaries were paid to the men from the commercial workshops. The stage manager employed by the commercial production company habitually complained that the low budget required cutting labour costs. The crew from the artistic team ultimately found ourselves commuting to the rehearsal studio to keep track of the ever-changing set requirements, and then going to the closed commercial workshops on a Sunday to make the stage sets ourselves. Disputes and dramatic expulsions occurred one after the other from this time on.

In 1986, *Aoi mi o tabeta* (Unripe fruits eaten) received the prestigious Kinokuniya Theatre Prize. That year was also the year for my dramatic expulsion.

The popularity of the theatre company and the brightness of performance on stage had grown inversely proportional over this eight-year period. Small theatre companies desperately tried to survive the commercial cogwheel which was in frenzied motion. A few years after I left the theatre company Japan's economy collapsed, many commercial workshops went bankrupt and the large number of minor theatre groups who had been pulled into the bubble economy stalled as a result of exhaustion. The name Aoitori survived, but it lost many members and much of the lustre to which I was originally attracted.

Despite all the unreasonable things that occurred, Aoitori was my "education". Buffered by absurdity, I developed rich friendships and acquired knowledge that couldn't be gleaned from books or personal biases while pursuing the mutual goal of creating theatre work. Most of the friends who encouraged me to go to Australia with Claire, and who looked after Nyan Nyan, were people with whom I'd cultivated friendships during this time.

After leaving the company, my life with Nyan Nyan returned to quietness. Looking as if she knew all my pleasures and pain, Nyan Nyan would sometimes gaze up at me. She was always on my side.

In the beginning, I think, as far as Claire was concerned, Nyan Nyan was nothing more than a cat I owned. To Nyan Nyan, Claire was a burdensome human. When I decided to go to Australia for a year I felt genuinely sorry that I must leave Nyan Nyan behind. Luckily for us, we had some close friends. Lesbian, gay and straight friends. Friends from the theatre company, friends from our band Kinbiren, clubbing friends, and snorkeling friends. Thanks to these friends, who took turns looking after her, Nyan Nyan made it through that year we were away.

I clearly remember the day I returned to my room in Tokyo after a year in Perth. Nyan Nyan sat in her chair with her back to me, staring out the window.

"Nyan, I'm home," I said as I walked toward her, but she continued to keep her back stiff, staring out the window ignoring me.

"Nyan, I'm back. Sorry for leaving you all alone." Even as I picked her up in my arms Nyan Nyan wouldn't look me in the eyes, she forcibly kept her face away from mine. That was the biggest show of resistance Nyan Nyan's small body could muster.

Returning to Tokyo, I was more relieved than anything that Nyan Nyan was still alive. When Claire wasn't home, I sometimes took Nyan Nyan's face in both hands and said, "Nyan you're alive. I'm so glad you're alive. Thank goodness you're alive."

Our life patterns had altered. Relations between Nyan Nyan and Claire, who had never quite been on good terms before Australia, also began to change. Claire and I would sit at our own desks in our small apartment room, working or studying. Nyan Nyan would sit under Claire's chair grooming herself. Sometimes the wheel of Claire's chair caught Nyan Nyan's tail. With a meow of resistance, a tuft of Nyan Nyan's tail sometimes got caught.

"That's why I told you not to sit there, Nyan Nyan." Claire would carry Nyan Nyan back to her own bed, but in no time Nyan Nyan would again be sitting under her desk. As if to offer moral support, Nyan Nyan sat comfortably purring while Claire wrote up research into the early morning hours. Nyan Nyan would sit near Claire, demand a share of her favorite *nori*, be fond of the smell of her clothing, even peep at her in the bath. Showing interest in Claire's behaviour became part of her day.

Nyan Nyan died of old age three years after we returned. She was almost twenty years old. In Japan they say cats like to die alone, that they hide themselves when they feel death approaching. Before her death, Nyan Nyan lost her appetite and had a series of convulsive fits. The vet, who made house calls, said old age had made her heart weak and that we should let her die quietly.

One cold autumn night Nyan Nyan tried to sneak outside when she knew I wasn't home. Claire intercepted her at the stairs. "If you go now you'll break Marou's heart." Claire tried to convince her to stay. Nyan Nyan, who hadn't eaten in several days, lay down and took a few sips of the strong coffee Claire had brought with her. The two of them sat outside on the cold concrete waiting for me. For the following week Claire and I took turns staying awake to look after Nyan Nyan. A few days later Nyan Nyan finally stopped breathing while I was holding her on our bed.

The friends who had cat-sat for Nyan Nyan were at her funeral at the Jikein temple. Nyan Nyan's body was placed in a small casket and cremated. Together we gathered the remaining bones and put them into the urn with her ashes.

"This is the tail."

"This is the hip bone."

"This is the head that you all patted." The monk explained each remaining bone and in groups of two we used ceremonial chopsticks to place them in the urn. The urn holding Nyan Nyan's remains was placed by the altar and, while the monk recited a sutra, each of us silently sprinkled incense and paid our respects. Leaving the funeral I noticed several anguished families awaiting their turn for their pet's cremation. Jikein temple, one of the few pet cemeteries in Tokyo, appeared to be doing good business.

Several telegrams of condolence arrived when I got home. I went to nearby Inokashira Park alone, and stared quietly up at the autumn sky stretching beyond the tall trees.

As anyone who has kept an animal for ten years or more knows, what may be merely a dog or a cat to any other person is a uniquely precious life. The shock of Nyan Nyan's death was greater than I expected: I didn't recover for the rest of that year. I was obsessed with the absurd desire for Nyan Nyan to come back to life. It was only when, on the anniversary of her death, I self-published a small book titled *Memories of Nyan Nyan*, that I was able to recover. Along with my own personal memories and Claire's, the book is filled with the memories of friends aged five to fifty who took care of Nyan Nyan. I discovered aspects of Nyan Nyan in it that I'd never known. After producing that small book I was able to shake my impossible wish of Nyan Nyan coming back to life.

I still worry, though, did Nyan Nyan ever forgive me?

Chapter 14

$\mathcal{L}ove$ THEORETICAL CURVES

I walked out of the doctor's room on crutches. Hesitantly, I glanced up at Marou. The look of shock on her face was almost comical.

"Oh, dear, so you really did do something to your knee?"

"Yep, the doctor said the way I fell overstretched the area. Perhaps even tore the ligament."

"What about the crutches?"

"The nurse said to post them back from Tokyo."

Marou and I arrived in Hokkaido, the north island, yesterday. It was my third time skiing. Ten years ago as an exchange student I'd attempted the slopes in Niigata. Fear of heights and my inability to control moving objects, like skis, had caused me to abandon the effort on the second day. Last December I'd spent four days with Marou in Furano. I'd taken ski lessons, then screamed my whole way up the ski lift. Yesterday, when we arrived in Niseko, I promised myself to make an improvement on last year.

"You can do it. You can do it. Left, right. Left, right." A year ago, I'd been so engrossed tackling the bottom half of the beginner's slope that I'd knocked Marou over and damaged her shoulder. This year, although we made it down the beginner's slope twice in two hours, the results were painful for me. My fear of heights hadn't disappeared, and to make it worse I still couldn't ski off the seat at the end of the lift.

"Stand up. Stand up. Lift your skis. You there, lift your skis."

"I would, if I could!" I screamed back. Suddenly the sky flipped over and I had snow in my mouth. My skis were tangled near my backside. I toppled over the final hump and into the safety barrage. Red danger flags fluttered behind me. Marou looked too surprised to laugh.

"Practise getting off before you come up next time," the lift operator grumbled as he came out of the control booth from where he had just stopped the whole line. I saw skiers, skis dangling over tree tops, waiting anxiously for the lift to move again. "If you can't get off, then you shouldn't be up here." He was shouting as he thrust out his hand to heave me out of the pile of snow.

"If you had a practice area I'd practise. I told the guy at the bottom I wasn't any good. All he said was 'No problem—take it slow.'" I hated not succeeding at slippery tasks: I always ended up crying just at the critical moment. As it happened now, I needed a five-minute rest to catch my breath and calm my fury before I could tackle the downhill again.

The scenery was breathtaking, if you could stand the height. A great arc of mountain carved into a wintry blue sky. Usually I couldn't stomach anything higher than a low ladder, so my survival tactic up here was to keep my eyes focused immediately in front of me. That way I could block out the frighteningly small specks of people swerving to the finish near the café below.

Forty sweaty minutes later, we arrived at the bottom. After our mammoth trek down the slope we were both tired. Marou suggested taking a break at the log café. The coffee had a comforting effect, and watching the talented skiers sparked my enthusiasm. Re-encountering the minus-four-degree cold outside, however, we both knew it was wisest to go home before we were totally exhausted. All that remained was to negotiate the gentle slope down to the carpark.

"Uh-ow. Shit." My bum plonked down between my legs, and I felt a pain shoot down the inside of my knee.

"What did you do?" Hearing me cry out, Marou turned around.

"I think I did something to my knee."

"You'll be alright." No big deal; perhaps. I took off my skis. I grew a little concerned, however, as I hobbled to the bus stop. I got even more worried when I couldn't move my leg the next morning. The manager of the log house complex drove Marou and me to the nearest hospital in Niseko. The X-ray process was painful, and the crutches prescribed were a first-time experience. Since childhood I'd been a faller. Mum says it was never a matter of if I would fall, but where I would fall. Apparently I left my mark daily on the footpath between our house and kindergarten. Amazingly, I'd never done anything daring enough to break any bones. Well, that was until I broke a rib doing mat-tumbles at high school phys-ed class in Saitama.

Although I was prone to falling down, I had been doing it dramatically the past few years. Two years earlier, just after I'd passed the entrance exams into the postgraduate course, I'd fallen between the platform and a train at Shibuya station. I must have missed my footing stepping onto the train. One minute I was standing, then the next thing the train floor was at eye level. My rucksack prevented me from falling further. Two men behind me hollered, "Watch out!" They hauled my body up onto the platform. Suddenly the music signalling the train's departure began to play; dazed, I stepped onto the train and felt the doors close behind me. The train took off in the direction of Harajuku.

In that instant the preceding events flashed through my mind. The way I figured it, Yamanote line trains only stop for approximately one minute at each station. If those guys behind me hadn't pulled me up, my head would be crushed on the rails right now.

"Um. Two hundred and fifty. I win again."

With my leg temporarily immobile, Marou had decided to stay off the slopes. We'd picked up fried chicken as a substitute Christmas feast, and were playing Uno to pass the time. The only slight problem was that I continued winning.

"Let's make it first to five hundred then." I suggested, and we continued with a couple more hands.

"Um, I'm on five hundred. Shall we extend a little bit more?"

"No. I'm going to have a bath." Marou busied herself filling the tub and experimenting with the sauna. From what I could tell, she wasn't particularly enjoying the day's events.

Our trip to the snow was a small indulgence. A month and a half after Nyan Nyan died, I submitted my master's thesis. I'd written the last month's worth of research on gender representation in Japanese-language bilingual dictionaries without Nyan Nyan's physical feline support. With a foldaway table stationed in the middle of our small room and surrounded by an ever growing stack of books, my impending deadline had dominated Marou's and my immediate life. The intermediate results would be posted in the last weeks of January. If I passed this initial stage I might be asked to defend my work, and if successful, accepted into the doctorate course. Since the whole visa kerfuffle six years ago, I didn't count on anything happening smoothly. It was too early for this trip to be an anticipatory celebration. Yet, as Marou and I were still grieving Nyan Nyan's death, a week in a log house in the snow was a great way to do away with unnecessary fretting.

At the interview Marou and I did with *Cosmopolitan* magazine at the end of January, I wore a long wool skirt to keep my leg warm. *Cosmopolitan* had read of our Joint Living Agreement in a lesbian magazine and wanted to include information on it in their feature on relationships. They considered the document an example of possible alternatives for couples, gay, lesbian or otherwise, in relationships which fell outside the marriage system. A few days after the magazine hit the shelves, I received a telephone call from the editorial staff. They had a fax from a woman who wanted to contact me. I was intrigued.

"Marou look. A fax from my high school friend." A group of friends from my Japanese high school had seen the article and the large photo accompanying it.

"See, I told you there was a reason for having that photograph taken." After a ten-year blank I met three of my school friends outside a huge new department store in Shinjuku. I was coming full circle. Kelly, my friend from Perth, had arrived in Tokyo months earlier. It was exciting sharing my Tokyo existence with my friend of twenty years. I felt supported by family and friends both near and afar. In the past six years I'd begun to pick up and hold pieces of the memory I'd scattered from here to Perth.

Three weeks before my reunion with my high school friends, I was accepted into the doctorate course. My scholarship was also extended. What had begun as a way to stay in Japan was becoming a passionate pursuit. With my thesis submitted, the dictionary project I had begun while at university in Perth was basically complete. Currently I was anxious to shift my attention to the linguistic interface of gender and sexuality. To tackle this I needed to situate myself more fully within my own work.

At the low-key graduation ceremony for the master's degree, a fellow student approached me. "Um. Were you interviewed in *Cosmopolitan* last week?"

"Yes." I smiled into his concerned eyes.

"My wife read it and showed it to me. I must say I was very shocked."

"Why thanks, I do believe we were the first same-sex couple to draw up legal documents like that."

I didn't bother asking what had shocked him the most, that I had been interviewed, or that for the past two years he'd regularly spoken with a "dyke". With the interview and photo I symbolically crossed another line which I'd previously let hold me back. In the past two years, since changing from the classical Japanese department to the postgraduate division, I'd gradually peeled away layer after layer of paranoid fear.

"Gee, they're great shoes," a colleague in the elevator commented.

"Thanks, I borrowed them from my partner. She has some really cool clothes."

"Oh, that's nice." I wondered if she missed the pronoun, or merely thought that a partner signalled business. Coming out or not coming out is hardly ever a decision consciously made. For those of us removed from the media limelight, it is an insidious process which never ends. Ultimately it depends on how the person we are talking to interprets the relevant statements.

A few weeks after the *Cosmopolitan* interview, I participated in a round-table discussion for *Gendai Shisō*, a well-read journal of "modern thought". A special volume on gay and lesbian studies was planned for the summer. Both Marou and I contributed to the issue edited by members of the gay and lesbian rights group Occur. Marou facilitated a discussion on the history of the lesbian community over the past three decades; I participated in a talk on the current state of lesbian and gay studies.

The academic world in Japan was opening to sexuality studies. Unfortunately a subtle divide between the subjects of study and everyday life still lingered. Influenced by my experiences in Tokyo, readings in lesbian studies and gay studies, and the increasing volume of work published under the name of queer studies, I felt urgency in putting emotion into the words of theory. Academic papers may just be drops in the water, but I knew that once I positioned myself there was no turning back. It was neither a luxury nor a privilege to hide my frustration at talks of sexuality which didn't acknowledge Japan's contemporary lesbian presence. After listening to Marou's recollections of Japanese lesbian history, I knew this was a cyclical process. Theories came, they would go. The continuing thread behind them was individual lives. Lives which are ultimately liked in some way to my own. Without the voice of lived experience, circumstances remain unchanged by the barrage of words which accompany every new phase.

In 1997 the political climate in Japan freezes with conservatism. The Kōbe earthquake of 1995, which claimed the lives of over 6300 people, and the terrorist sarin gas attack on Tokyo subways have left an indelible effect. The governments of the United States and Japan forge ahead with renegotiating security guidelines, oblivious to grassroots activists demanding debate. The recession breeds widespread economic conservatism, and employment figures indicate that young women increasingly are finding it more difficult to secure work than their male counterparts. In academia, theories founded solely in English and imbued with purely Western historical frameworks are inadequate. Reverting to orientalist discourses robs my lover of her words. We need discourse that will engage the contradictions abounding in contemporary political climates. In Tokyo, lesbians must, and do, continue placing our own words into the milieu and demanding a voice.

Chapter 15

MOVING

After Nyan Nyan died, Claire passed her final master's degree examinations and made her debut into the world of theory. We continued to live in the apartment room situated three minutes walk from Kichijōji station—a Tokyo town filled with restaurants, cafés, boutiques and department stores. From the south-east corner window of our one-room, wooden-floored apartment we could glance at the sky, something of a rarity in Tokyo. We shared the top third floor with a karate office and, except when the cherry blossoms were in bloom and people poured into Inokashira Park down the road, the area was relatively uncrowded. It was a pleasant room for two people to share.

However, as Claire prepared for her doctoral dissertation and I began working on a book on old Japanese *Chanbara* films, the time we spent at our desks and the number of accompanying documents began to increase. The inconveniences of this room of thirty square metres became increasingly obvious. It was too small to party in with friends. Grilling fish was prohibited when the washing was hanging out on the curtain racks. Nyan Nyan's claw prints were scratched on the white walls; but Nyan Nyan was no longer with us. Over a couple of years, too, the once quiet area around our apartment had begun to change. Situated just three minutes from the town's major shopping area, a cram-school, business college and McDonald's opened in close succession. Gradually larger numbers of young people flocked to the area. There were no school grounds at either of the complexes, so cram-school and business college students sat in groups on the road during their breaks. When they left, polystyrene trays littered with leftovers, disposable chopsticks, cans and paper scattered the street. In the early morning, scavenging crows circled in the sky. Late into Saturday nights the street transformed into a hangout for straight kids hoping to pick each other up.

"Let's move soon, shall we?" I was the first one to mention looking for a new apartment.

"Okay, if we find somewhere we really like." Claire wasn't enthusiastic about moving. I didn't know why.

None of the properties registered with the real estate agencies that we investigated were suitable. An apartment close to the station was situated above a noisy *Pachinko* parlour. A so-called "superior apartment complex" had long narrow rooms with only one window. At one complex a nosy-looking caretaker paced around the lobby. Another building had huge cracks in the concrete which surely would not withstand the force of a major earthquake. Claire and I visited a small house at the end of a tiny laneway that got no sun and smelt of damp, apartments occupied by a religious sect, a heavily overpriced new complex, a small room situated above a 24-hour deli. We did find a relatively new apartment which was forty metres square, but there was no point in moving to a place not much bigger than where we already lived. If we looked for somewhere in the older areas of Tokyo near the river, or new residential areas located inconveniently far from the central Tokyo district, we might have had more luck. But, above everything, we wanted to stay in Kichijōji and have access to the park.

One day we'd spent hours visiting local real estate agencies when we finally found an apartment in which we were interested. It was a compromise of sorts. The real troubles began now we had discovered a place into which we might want to move. It was a two-bedroom apartment managed by a cooperative union. Thirty minutes walk from Kichijōji station, the total floor space was the least we were willing to compromise on. The roof terrace of sixty square metres adjoining the bright fourth-floor corner room was the main attraction. Tokyo rivalled only New York and London for lack of space and price of living, so a spacious roof terrace was attractive. The room itself was small, but we could still invite friends over for a roof garden party.

"We'd very much like to rent this room," I said, worried that the reply would be *gaijin* weren't welcome. In an act of unusual fairness, the real estate agent phoned the owner on the spot.

"Oh, really? Of course. I see." After a brief conversation the agent put down the receiver and turned to me, "Um, the owner says that he will only rent the apartment to married couples with young children, or couples who are planning on getting married in the near future."

"What?"

"Why is that?"

"Well, the owner only wants to rent to people who have the same lifestyle as the current residents. He wants to avoid *trouble*. If there is any *trouble* the owner will be put in a spot, and he wants to avoid that situation."

"What do you mean by *trouble*?"

"Hmm, well, everyone has to be on the same footing."

"We intend to live within the limits of common sense, of course."

"Yes, well, the owner only wants to rent to married couples or young families …"

Claire scraped the chair loudly as she got up from her seat. "Yes, I understand. We wouldn't want to live in such an environment anyway."

We left the real estate agency with grim faces. We entered another real estate agency on the other side of the station. An apartment complex managed by a famous department store chain caught our eye. The room seemed to get quite a lot of sunshine— a major consideration in humid Tokyo—and the size wasn't too bad. It was reasonably close to the station, and within our price range. The whole apartment complex appeared to be reasonably sturdy. It was a middle-range option and a vast improvement on other complexes we'd seen. We decided to negotiate for a contract.

The estate agent was friendly and surprisingly seemed to understand how difficult it was for foreigners to find accommodation in Japan. But he sighed when I mentioned the property in which we were interested. "That apartment, yes, I see. The company which owns it won't rent unless the potential occupants have an annual salary in excess of six million yen. There was a young couple here yesterday who desperately wanted that apartment, but unfortunately they didn't have the required salary."

"We have that salary combined."

"Yes, but in your case, you are only friends. One of you alone must fit the required salary bracket."

I jumped at the words "friends". "Why is that?"

"If one of you vacates, then the other won't be able to pay the rent, will she? There is always a lot of trouble for that reason."

That word again: "trouble". Claire and I looked at each other. "But we *are* family!" I wanted to scream.

"So many people do it. So many people cause trouble by suddenly vacating and not keeping up rental payments."

"Yes, but you never know when a married couple might get divorced either, do you? And so many companies are downsizing, you never know when a salaried businessman might lose his job either, eh?" I interrupted immediately. It backfired.

"Oh no, the level of commitment between friends and family is incomparable. A married couple is completely different to a couple of friends living together, whatever do you mean?" This real estate agent would rent a property to a married couple or blood relations with no problems whatsoever, as he continued to explain. The words "But Claire and I are family, we have a legal agreement, you can trust us as people too" rose up into my mouth as I listened to him drone on. I had to force those words to the back of my throat. Your average real estate agent would react to the scandalous nuances of our being "queer" and throw us out of the shop if I said anything like that. I couldn't tell him that we were partners, because if he was a real estate agent who wouldn't rent properties to friends he surely wouldn't rent to a couple of queers. I was silenced by the system which banished us to its periphery.

Claire stood up and kicked her chair in. "Thank you very much for your time. I am impressed that for the sake of some piddly apartment you lecture on about salaries, rental conditions and family." Claire left the agency in a huff. The agent sat with mouth wide open.

It might be difficult to believe but, out of all the agencies we visited, these last two were the most helpful. In most cases we were turned away because they didn't rent to foreigners; or because they didn't rent to occupants who weren't registered on the same *koseki* (family register)—that is, either legally married, blood relatives or adopted relatives; or because they wouldn't rent to a woman who worked freelance. We had all the right qualifications for being turned away.

"I wasn't enthusiastic about moving for this very reason. I really didn't want us to get hurt again."

"Let's forget it."

"I don't want to visit another real estate agency. But I might give the Internet a try." Resigned to the inevitable, Claire sent details of our budget, the type and area of rental property in which we were interested to a property information centre operating for foreign residents. We stopped visiting real estate agencies and didn't mention the prospect of moving again.

"What on earth is this?" A fax arrived a few days later from an unknown company. It showed floor plans, addresses and rent figures. I'd put all thoughts of moving completely out of my mind and it took me a while to realise that these were potential rental properties. The company Claire had accessed on the Internet had contacted us. By the look of the fax, the company dealt mostly in "executive apartments" for foreign residents. However, among these highly priced "executive" apartments was the floor plan for a property about twenty minutes from our apartment. We went to check it out the next day.

It was a small terrace house located in a quiet residential area. A few old Japanese-style homes still stood near by. By the look of it, it was a residential area for people with a bit of extra money—one house was surrounded by a magnificent fence of trees, another timber-framed house had a traditional Japanese garden not seen much any more, and the house opposite had a strangely unique architectural design. When we first saw the small, white, two-storey duplex house, Claire and I looked at each other and sighed. It was completely different to any of the other properties we had visited. Situated fifteen minutes walk from Kichijōji station, it was also bright and sunny.

"Are we in the right place?" We'd seen a range of mostly horrible-looking complexes and I still couldn't believe this was it. The minute I opened the small entrance gate I liked the place. The step into the house from the entrance hall was just the right height for taking off your shoes. The rooms were unusually open for Tokyo, and the stairwell extended up to the ceiling. Sunlight streamed through the bay windows. A Japanese-style wooden bath pail would fit in well with the bathroom, and best of all there was a small garden attached. This house was minute by Australian standards, but it had a wonderful atmosphere.

At last, a house I'd like to live in, Claire seemed to be saying to herself. What she finally said was "I really love this house, but I think it is a little out of our price range. If the rent was reduced a bit we would sign a rental agreement immediately."

Ueno, the man from the real estate agency, pulled down a set of hidden stairs to show off the storage space in the roof and smiled. "I can marginally reduce the advertised price." He seemed to have no doubt that we could rent this house.

"How is that possible?"

Ueno answered our question briefly. "Because of the bubble bursting, and the recession, this property has been unoccupied for more than six months. If you can sign the rental contract immediately, I will reduce the price. Leave the negotiation with the owners to me." Claire's nationality was no problem because this real estate agent dealt in properties for foreign residents. He didn't ask anything about our relationship. There was no problem either when I admitted I worked freelance. Even if it meant cutting their profit margins, it seemed they were anxious to rent. The recession made this all possible. The only condition was that we sign the contract that week and supply a total of seven months rent in advance—two months deposit, two months key money, this month's rent, next month's rent and a month's rent in estate agency fees. Luckily I had just received a lump-sum insurance payment. It was all a matter of chance. Claire, Ueno and I happily signed a preliminary agreement.

We had cleared three difficult hurdles, but there was still a fourth condition we needed to fulfil: the problem of a guarantor and their registered seal. Seals—that is stamps engraved with the bearer's name—fulfil the same function as signatures. Individual seals are registered at the local municipal office and used on official legal documents. When renting in Japan, it is usual for occupants to provide a character reference, commonly known as a guarantor, and present copies of the card certifying the guarantor's registered seal. In some instances it was also necessary to provide details of the financial standing of the proposed guarantor.

I reflected back on the thirty years I'd lived in Tokyo. Why had I never had any problems renting apartments or houses? Then it dawned on me: until now, whenever I rented I had always written my father's name as the guarantor and used one of his seals. I had never seriously thought about having to prove the worth of my character. Without being aware of it, as a native-born Japanese and the daughter of a doctor who ran his own private hospital, I'd always been in a secure position. I had rebelled against the power my father held in the world, but at the same time benefited from it.

The public confidence placed in doctors was particularly strong. In the 1970s, for example, the police undertook an investigation aimed at flushing out terrorist groups like Ōkami no Kiba ("fangs of the wolf") and Sekigunha ("the red army") who targeted national corporations. The police came to the apartment where I lived by myself to question me. I had just become acquainted with the lesbian feminists and frequented the printing press at the radical women's lib commune Libsen which we were renting to make our first dyke newsletter. The doorbell rang and I opened the door to a short, shrewd-looking man who jammed his foot in the doorway and flashed police identification from the inside of his suit pocket. He had his foot in the door so I couldn't close it on him when he tried to enter.

"I'm with the police."

"Yes."

"I have some questions. Answer them."

"Yes."

This so-called policeman first asked a series of detailed questions about my birthplace, my major at university and work, and then struck up a conversation about current affairs. Finally he asked, "So you said you are from Kyoto, right?" He repeated this several times. Each time I replied, "No. I'm from Gifu." After four or five repetitions I got sick of giving the same answer. "How many times do you need to ask? I'm from Gifu. *Gifu*. I was born in Gifu!"

His eyes shone. "Hmmm. I see. You aren't from Kyoto then. What does your family do?"

"Doctor. My father runs a hospital."

"Oh, a doc, doctor? Your father is a doctor? What is the name of the hospital?" He suddenly became flustered. I gave him the name of the hospital. I also feigned small talk and gave him the name of a well-known politician my father worked with behind the scenes.

"Oh dear. I am terribly sorry. I had no idea. Sorry, sorry." He suddenly changed tone. "Actually, the married couple next door got in contact with us. They said that you didn't seem to be married, that there was often a light on until the early hours of the morning, and that many people seemed to congregate here. They think you are rather suspicious. I came to investigate their claims. Sorry to have troubled you." Bowing numerous times, he slid away.

I wonder how long the police would have continued questioning me if I hadn't used my father's occupation and name-dropped his political connections? I didn't think anything about it at the time. I loathed my father's authority, but I was also secured by it. I could even use it to get rid of a high-handed police officer.

The father I rebelled against is longer with us; he died of old age over a year ago. For the first time my father's death seemed real. For years I had continued to live under his hidden protection. If a guarantor and registered seal are necessary to rent a room, that means there are people who can't rent rooms. Now it was apparent that I might well be one of those refused. I realised for the first time the lines of discrimination of which I had previously been unaware.

"Can you ask a professor to be your guarantor?" Ueno made this suggestion when I told him both my parents were dead. "The owner said that if your guarantor is a professor there will be no problem."

The university that Claire attended commanded at least as much public trust as a doctor. Just hearing its name people would prostrate as if face to face with the imperial family's chrysanthemum crest. It was a symbol of ridiculous authority. We had to try using it if we wanted to rent this house.

"Oh, dear. I suppose I'll ask and see." Claire said she'd approach her academic supervisor, but she didn't seem enthusiastic. There were a large number of foreign students at university. It was unlikely that a professor would become her guarantor as a special favour to her.

Surprisingly, Claire's academic supervisor said he would gladly do it. However, on the appointed day when Claire returned to her supervisor's office to sign the papers, there was a hitch. He had read over the copy of the contract agreement

Claire had left with him. According to the contract, a guarantor for two people was necessary. I was noted as the tenant, Claire as the sub-tenant. Claire's supervisor was extremely apologetic when he explained he would gladly be her guarantor, but there was no way he could act as guarantor for Ms Izumo whom he had never met. It had been a wild shot: he was totally within reason to refuse our request.

When Claire finally rang me that day she sounded very depressed. "Looks like we'll have to give up the idea of moving." We discussed this a little, before I hung up. The phone rang again. It was my good friend Mōko. We chatted for a while before she asked, "Are you going to move?"

"Well, I want to, but we can't find anyone to act as guarantor. We're actually in a bit of a fix at the moment."

"A guarantor? I can do it if you like."

"Really?"

"Yeah, it's no problem. But will they approve of me? I work freelance after all."

"Yeah, I have no idea. But I'll ask the real estate agent. Thanks, as always."

Ueno placed the key he had expected to hand to us beside him and shook his head, distressed. I had already paid over one million yen.

"Would a freelance editor be acceptable for our guarantor?"

"Let me ask the owner."

I telephoned Mōko and asked her to fax a copy of her tax statements. Ueno faxed them to the owner. Sipping green tea, we waited for the reply. It was a slow thirty minutes. I watched Kichijōji slip into darkness from the office window. The agent had a property he wanted to rent, we wanted to rent it, and although we had already paid a huge deposit we still couldn't move in. We had cleared all kinds of hurdles until this. If we couldn't pass this final obstacle and the whole deal fell through, there was nothing to do but put it down to bad luck. Ueno's smiling face interrupted my thoughts. The result was an okay. All we need now was certification of Mōko's registered seal.

The next day Claire and I woke with excitement.

"Paradise certainly does begin with friends," Claire said looking happy.

The telephone rang. It was Mōko. She'd visited the ward office first thing that morning, but couldn't get a certificate copy of her seal registration with the identification papers she had. The copy of her insurance card that she'd submitted didn't rate for approval for a same-day issue; either a driver's licence or a passport was required. Mōko's passport was out of date, and she didn't drive. The only other option was for someone with a certificate of seal registration to accompany her to the ward office and act as her guarantor.

"Okay. I'll be there as fast as I can." I was about to become Mōko's guarantor to enable her to become the guarantor for Claire and I. It was a complicated state of affairs. By the afternoon, the certificate showing Mōko's seal registration was ready. I jumped onto the subway back to Kichijōji with this in my hands. At the Kichijōji real estate agency we stamped our seals on the multi-paged rental agreement in the presence of a licensed mediator. By the time we finally had the front door key in our hands, the winter sun had set and the day was over.

The terrorist group Ōkami no Kiba inadvertently set off the bomb they were making in an accident which led to their arrests. They rented the apartment they used by presenting themselves as "normal people"—a salaried man and his wife. This police department's pathetic anti-terrorist operations had not tracked them down. The "normal couple" pulled up the apartment's floorboards and made a secret basement where they prepared explosives. Comments from their neighbours were published in the mass media following the couple's arrest. "They were very quiet, normal people. I didn't think anything strange about them at all."

The members of Ōkami no Kiba knew if they wore the mask of normality, this vague social concept would enable them to smoothly carry out plans against Japanese society and launch a terrorist attack. In the twenty-five years since the 1970s era of terrorism, anti-government, youth, and brutal sexual crimes have increased in Japan. When perpetrators are arrested, news broadcasts show comments from the neighbours. "He was a such a quiet type. I can't believe he would do something as horrible as this."

Every time a comment like that is broadcast, Claire sneers at the TV screen: "No-one is as suspect as a *normal*-looking person."

I am writing this from the second-floor room of the house we moved into. Claire is sleeping in the room across the hall after a day at university. Photos of our family and friends are on display on the bookcase in our work room. A breeze fragrant with summer is blowing through the window. This house is very quiet and comfortable.

This is the quiet that always follows as Claire and I traverse the exclusion we cyclically encounter.

Afterword

$\mathcal{L}_{OV\mathcal{E}}$ (R)EVOLUTION AT NAGARAGAWA

The Chūō line platform at Tokyo station has been redeveloped. The escalators are now on steep inclinations. I make Marou walk with me to the stairs at the end. Thankfully the architects reserved an alternative for those of us who can't stand heights. That day I almost ran down the multi-level staircase in my excitement to get to the bullet train.

Gifu. Marou and I were going to Gifu.

Nagaragawa Hotel sat quietly facing Nagaragawa. One of the few rivers left in its natural state in Japan, it flowed rapidly, ignoring the rows of four-wheel-drives invading its banks. Day trippers with expensive portable barbecues and blue plastic sheets swarmed on the edge of the water. Some kids in bathers and goggles bobbed their heads up and down looking for fish. It was a pseudo-camping area without adequate garbage facilities.

As we rode over the bridge in the taxi, my heart rose a little from where it had slumped. Grey skies and concrete. With a bit of imagination Nagaragawa could be the Swan River, and the overlooking mountain with the castle, Kings Park. The problem was, I didn't feel imaginative. Marou's mood had obviously altered when we changed to the Meitetsu line at Nagoya station.

After an hour of deep sighing, we dragged our bags out of the taxi and into the hotel lobby.

Today marked the end of mourning. Marou's father had died a month ago. After being pumped full of air and resuscitated numerous times, he was finally allowed to take his last breath. During the two weeks Marou spent in and out of Gifu prior to his death, I plunged into negativity. It was as if my existence had been cancelled out in the part of the world she now occupied. We made clandestine telephone calls, the first of which prompted me to race around Kichijōji looking for clothes suitable for the inevitable funeral.

"Hello. May I please speak to Marou." My heart pounded into the receiver. All I could hope was that, when I rang to tell her I'd posted the clothes, her sister-in-law wouldn't hang up.

The lobby of the Nagaragawa Hotel had a gaudy chandelier. Some of the greyish-white chairs in the restaurant-cum-bar angled to the river. We checked in at reception and were shown across the salmon-coloured carpet to an elevator leading to our room. The *tatami* was a little worn, but the room itself as comfortable as other Japanese-style hotels. A low table occupied the centre, where "welcome cakes" had been placed alongside green tea. The *nakai* assigned to our room poured tea and briefly introduced the hotel amenities. Marou's family gathering would begin shortly and I would be left on my own. Alone in Marou's home town. I waved her goodbye and tried not to think about what her brother might say when she asked if he'll meet me. Exhausted by nervous excitement, I lay down on the *tatami* and attempted to sleep.

Twenty minutes later pop music pumped out from speakers lining the river. A cormorant fishing show was scheduled for tonight. Did they have to announce it with such trashy music?

Dragging a comb through my hair, I checked the watch on my other wrist. At least another hour and a half until Marou's family dinner finished. I decided to go for a walk to check out the four-wheel-drives on the river bank. But first, I thought I'd see what restaurants there were.

I got off the elevator at the second floor. Poking my head down the corridor I noticed the banquet rooms. Hmm, the Izumo family are having a reception here tonight. … Wait a minute, the Izumo family? A dinner reception here? Marou had planned for us to stay at the hotel her family didn't usually book. Did she get her hotels messed up? I had better sneak out inconspicuously. What if her family happened to see me—not that they knew what I look like, nor I them, but a blonde in Gifu would surely raise their suspicions.

The river bank provided a nice walk. Grey pebbles and larger stones massaged my feet. Gentle pain was a fitting stimulant. A little more hungry when I got back, I rang reception, left a message of where I was going. I took the lift to the top floor to enjoy a lonely meal. The cormorant fishing show caused quite a commotion on the waterfront. The lead boat snaked along the river with a gaggle of cormorants at its bow. Spotting a sweetfish, the birds ducked into the water and scooped it into their beaks. Back at water level, the fishermen extracted the sweetfish from the cormorants' gullets. Apparently this form of fishing had a history of over a thousand years. Last century, the sweetfish these birds caught were placed on the imperial table. Now you can buy them in cold packs to take home as souvenirs.

The family eating at the table next to me masked my view of the river. From where I sat I could barely see the lead boats. The visible fleet of tourist boats which tailed them were certainly impressive. Halfway through my final coffee, Marou entered the restaurant.

"I've been looking for you all over."

"But I told reception I was up here."

"My brother and his wife are waiting downstairs." She smiled. I panicked and skated down to our room to change clothes.

"What should I wear? What should I wear?" Suddenly I hated every garment I had stuffed into our backpack.

"You look fine," Marou replied.

As I smudged off some of my lipstick for a more neutral tone, a thousand thoughts flickered through my brain. Marou and I made this a week-long trip. Just in case her brother angrily exploded telling us never to set foot in Gifu again, we arranged to drive up to the world heritage area and enjoy the thatched cottages in the countryside after the ceremonies. Soon I would know how much emphasis to place on that leg of our journey. My palms sweated profusely as I walked across the salmon-coloured lobby. With controlled calm, I stepped onto the sloping hotel driveway.

Marou's brother and his wife stood hand in hand, staring down at the river. The scene was cinematic, perfect lighting and no need for editing. Their silhouettes etched into my mind. I crossed the road with Marou. Smiling, we exchanged pleasantries. The final cormorant procession was doing its concluding turn. Suddenly the sky was alight with fireworks.

Some of our mutual stress dissipated as we drank coffee together after the fireworks display. I sat across from Marou's brother and marvelled at the familiarities which cross between generations, only to manifest themselves differently in sibling embodiments. I look a lot like my two sisters, and my brother, too. But we are each of us unique, sharing the shape of hands that go on to do different and separate things. Looking at Marou's brother, I wondered how personalities could waver towards similarity only to diverge into opposites. Luckily, my family offers support. I was unsure how this meeting would work out.

"So, I'll come over to the house in the morning." The following day Marou was to visit the family grave. Her father's urn would eventually join her brother and mother who had died more than ten years ago.

"Would Claire like to come with you?" Her sister-in-law breathed words that I was surprised to hear.

"Thank you, that would be wonderful." It was decided.

As we drove through the main town in the taxi the next morning I tried to concentrate on the sky. Perth skies consoled me; perhaps the Gifu blue would set me at ease the same way. We stopped to buy flowers. Marou bought a subdued selection to place near the urn which is still in her family's living room, and chrysanthemums which are traditionally placed at altars and graves. I bought a bouquet to give to her sister-in-law.

I crunched across the driveway gravel. Marou's family house was a monstrous construction. Stuffed birds in mid-flight perched in the living room alcove. Marble was spread through a section of the entrance hall. Once inside, Marou's sister-in-law gestured for me to sit in front of the huge photo of Marou's father. A giant stuffed cat was on one side, the family altar which housed photos of her brother and mother on the other. I put my hands together and lowered my head. For the first time in our relationship, I made acquaintance with Marou's mother and father.

Acquaintance through death; if it wasn't for this old man dying, I would never be in this house. Living in Tokyo, I missed the funerals of both my Grandma and my Pop. Sitting staring at the giant cat, I felt that grief wash over me again. In my mind's eye lies the last image I have of my other grandmother, Nana, and am thankful again that I could wish her goodbye. I have missed other family events: weddings, births, new jobs, graduations, business failures and successes. I know I will miss more. I cope by banishing lost memories from my mind, by using the telephone sparingly. Unfortunately, with the advent of email and lower phone charges, my effort to ignore the pain of distance by forgetting grows increasingly difficult.

Coming full circle, I alternate between the skies of Tokyo and Perth. I float between the land of summer greens, and the red earth that is my birth land. Oscillating between the two, the space I inhabit is neither, but perhaps in both. With Marou I have rediscovered the beauty of red earth, and concrete. Writing these chapters has made me appreciate again how lucky I am to experience that space daily, and the support of friends and family in both.

Writing and translating is not a solitary effort. It is collaborative. I thank Izumo Marou for her patience throughout our collaboration. Also, thanks to all at Spinifex Press for their efforts in getting this book published, Renate Klein, Nikki Anderson, Michelle Freeman, Maralann Damiano and especially to Susan Hawthorne for many years of invaluable editorial advice. Thanks to Janet Mackenzie for her editing expertise and Tracey Anne O'Mara for her cover design. I am also grateful for Sarah Teasley's readings and invaluable comments and Tsukamoto Yosuyo's helpful information.

There are many people who have enabled the writing and translating of this book. I am indebted to everyone who has allowed me to use our experiences in its pages. Needless to say, what I have written is subjective fragments of my own memory.

Some names have been altered for both personal and political reasons.

I would especially like to thank my family and friends, particularly my mum and dad for sending me away as an exchange student and leading me to courage. I am indebted to the words of support, the understanding and smiles of Hilary, Katherine, Jason, Russell, Ashley, Natalie, Jessica, Cameron, Alysha, Amy and Matilda. I would like to thank Kelly for over twenty years of warm friendship in Perth and Tokyo, Nikki and Terri for guiding and supporting me for many years, and Kath, Trish and others for new friendships. Also to Kumi, for a friendship developed beyond the office, and to Shu Lea, for collaborative genius and friendship. I wish to say thanks to my host families for welcoming me into their homes, and my friends at high school in Saitama for giving a base. To many friends, especially Horikawa, Ishiwatari, Kaori, Kazuko, Kawai, Kino, Makoto, Miyamoto, Miho, Miyazuka, Miwa, Mōko, Motojima, Ogi, Okajima, the Sano sisters, Sōji, Tsuchihashi, Tsutsumi, Ueno and Yumiko, thanks for financial support and emotional feeding. Also to Chū, Nagae, Guchi, Kayo, Kazuko, Mayuki and all other members, thanks for IBU. Finally, to the Tokyo lesbian and gay community, the Japanese queer community, thank you for accepting me and allowing me to participate in the struggle.

Afterword

When I met Claire, I didn't even know about Sydney's Gay and Lesbian Mardi Gras. I had never seen a gay or lesbian person march with their family at a pride march. For years I had many lesbian friends, but I'd never heard of any of them coming out to their family. There had never been a lesbian and gay march in Japan. That phenomenon has occurred like a linking wave in the past few years. A period coinciding with meeting Claire, and my return to Tokyo after a year with her in Australia.

Since returning to Tokyo, Claire and I have spent time in Perth at least once every two years. Absorbed in work, study, special events, or just having fun in Tokyo, I suddenly feel exceedingly homesick for Perth's parched seasons. At times like this one of us eventually says, "Let's go home to Perth soon."

This year, after enjoying the Sydney Gay and Lesbian Mardi Gras, we flew to Perth and spent a few weeks in a holiday apartment at Scarborough Beach. A week after we arrived, it was my birthday. The day before, Claire's brother's girlfriend bought over a joint present for me. For my birthday, Claire's mother and father, her two sisters and their husbands and children, her aunts, uncle and cousin brought home-made delights and gifts to our hotel apartment. We ate and talked all afternoon at this barbecue gathering. Among the presents I received were special handwritten cards that Claire's nieces and nephews had made. That day I felt immeasurable happiness at being a member of Claire's family.

I remember clearly the first time Claire's parents wrote me the word "family". It was in the card they sent me when my father died. It was signed "From your family in Perth". Reading that message lifted any depression I felt at the time. My birthday was as special for me as when I read that card. I was never close to my father, even up to his death, and it is precious to experience the loving thoughtfulness of Claire's family.

After the lunch party, Claire and I went to the nearby café to have coffee with her mother and father. With cappuccinos and espressos in front of us, for a while we four sat silently watching the beautiful sun set into the ocean off Scarborough Beach. Moment by moment the face of the sky altered with the ever moving clouds and tilting of the sun. No matter how many times I see it, whenever I see it, I never tire of Perth's sunset.

Claire's father asked me a philosophical question about the sunset. It was rather difficult to answer. At the café I became distinctly aware that Claire's philosophical side resembled her father's. Watching Claire talk with her mother and father about sexuality peacefully, neither raging nor indignant, I thought it one of the most amazing scenes of all. It was not possible for me to develop a trusting relationship with my father that would enable a discussion about sexuality. Now, having lost both of my parents, enacting the same scene is for ever impossible.

The first chapters of this book (Chapters 1, 3, 4, 6, 7) are translations of chapters rewritten from the book of the same title *Manaita no ue no koi* (Love upon the chopping board) published in 1993 by Takarajimasha. In this English version published with

Spinifex Press I have incorporated two major changes. One is the addition of essays written by Claire Maree. The other is essays focusing on "events after"—events which occurred during the "gay boom" period of the 1990s after Claire and I returned from Australia.

Several years have passed since talk of an English edition began, and as a result of that time, and my not checking reference sources until the last minute, I have caused great pains to my translator and co-author Claire Maree. I offer here my very special thanks to Claire for her work in both translation and writing while juggling her own research writing and presentations.

I thank all of the staff at Spinifex Press who made this English publication possible.

While in Australia I was fortunate not only to receive support from Claire's family, but to feel their love as they watched over my relationship with Claire. I wish to express my thanks and love to her mother and father and all of her family. Special thanks to Jeanette, Kevin, Hilary, Russell, Katherine, Ashley, Jason, Natalie, Susan and Linda.

Thanks to Kelly for being a conversation partner to my poor English. To Nikki for welcoming Claire and I warmly into her house. To Terri, also, for letting us stay with her. To Trish and Kath for sharing their experiences. To Ruth and Jo for taking part in interviews. To those friends who financially supported our trip to Australia, and took care of Nyan Nyan: Itō Lee, Okajima Mikiko, Ogi Akira, Kakuta Miho, Sasaki Toshiko, Motojima Kazumi, Sanō Hidemi, Tsutsumi Kuniko, Tsuchihashi Toshiko, Horikawa Makiko, Matsunaga Mōko, Minowa Eiko, Miyazuka Mayumi, Miyamoto Kazumi, Mori Yae, Yoshida Sōji. I really do thank you. I also offer thanks to Kawai Minato who choreographed the dance routines that *Kokusai Bian Renmei* performed at the first and second Lesbian and Gay Parades. Thank you for guiding us with passion in wind and in rain.

Thanks, also, to the gay and lesbian rights group Occur, and to my lawyer Nakagawa.

Finally, despite the "gay boom" which the mass media created in the 1990s, there are still lesbians who are battered and beaten by their fathers because of their sexuality. As a result of "trendy TV dramas", "normal" youth increasingly perpetrate gay-bashing crimes. I am fortunate to have found great happiness even in the midst of these cold-blooded events and the exclusion that Claire and I have encountered.

恋 GLOSSARY OF JAPANESE TERMS

Aoi Festival: The festival held at Shimogamo Shrine in Kyoto during May.

boku: A first-person pronoun generally explained as being used by boys and young men, or older men in casual conversation.

chanbara: A sword battle. *Chanbara* films have samurai themes and feature sword fights.

Edo period: The Japanese historical period extending from 1603 to 1867 when the capital was moved from Kyoto to Tokyo (then called Edo). Also known as the Tokugawa period.

fusuma: A papered sliding door used to partition rooms.

gaijin (lit. outside person): Common term for foreigners, especially for residents of Japan of white European heritage.

gaisen: A slang term referring to Japanese women or men who date or sleep exclusively with foreigners.

Hanafuda: Japanese playing cards which feature natural themes and calligraphy.

hanami: Cherry blossom viewing. In spring when the cherry-trees blossom, people flock into scenic areas and many hold picnic parties under the branches.

janken: The game of "paper, rock and scissors" which is both used to decide turns and played as a game.

Kabuki: A form of popular theatre originated as an alternative style by Izumo no Okuni in the late Momoyama period (1590–1603).

koseki: The family register system where all members of a household are registered according to birth date, and/or marriage date, and relationship to the head of the house— traditionally the husband and father. Most women who legally marry enter their names on their husband's register; if they divorce, their name is struck out with a cross. Unmarried women are usually registered under their father's registry, unless they remove themselves to form their own personal register.

Mama: A term of endearment used for managers of small bars.

mike: Japanese tortoiseshell cat with white, black and brown patterning.

miso: Soybean paste. *Miso* soup is served with most Japanese homestyle meals.

nagauta: A form of song accompanied by the *shamisen*.

nakai: A kimono-clad parlourmaid. A *nakai* is assigned to each room of a Japanese-style inn or hotel.

Ni-chōme: see Shinjuku Ni-chōme.

Nihon buyō: A traditional form of Japanese dance.

Noh: A form of classical Japanese theatre which had its roots in the Kamakura period (1185–1333).

nori: Thin slices of *laver* (seaweed), often toasted and seasoned.

obi: Sash worn with kimono.

okama: A derogatory term for male homosexuality and "effeminate" men. It has recently been reclaimed by some cross-dressing men, queers and drag queens.

omae: A second-person singular pronoun generally explained as being used by higher-status speakers to those of lower status, or by men to women.

onabe: A derogatory term for cross-dressing lesbian or transgender women. It has recently been reclaimed by some cross-dressing women, and drag kings.

onigiri: Savoury rice balls.

ore: A first-person pronoun generally explained as being used by men in casual or rough conversation.

pachinko: Pinball played for goods illegally exchanged for money. *Pachinko* parlours are clustered around most train stations.

rāmen: Noodles in a hot broth.

sake: Rice wine.

seiza: Sitting straight, on one's knees.

shamisen: Three-stringed instrument.

Shinjuku ni-chōme (also referred to as Ni-chōme): Small area of Shinjuku ward in central Tokyo, where bars, clubs, and recently some cafés, run for or by gays and lesbians are concentrated.

shitsurei shimasu: "Excuse me."

Shōwa era: The period from 1926 to 1989.

sukiyaki: A hotpot dish made with thinly sliced beef and vegetables cooked in a thick soya sauce broth.

Takarazuka: The famous all-woman revue theatre company.

tatami: Woven straw mats used as flooring in Japanese rooms.

Taishō era: The pre-war period from 1912 to 1926.

tōrō: The act of visiting a brothel.

washi: A first-person pronoun generally explained as being used by older men, especially in rural environments.

watashi: A first-person pronoun generally explained as being used in formal situations, and also by women in both casual and formal situations.

yakuza: Gangsters; Japanese "mafia".

Yoshiwara: Famous entertainment area formed when tea-houses and brothels were forcibly gathered into the same area during the Edo period.

OTHER BOOKS FROM SPINIFEX PRESS

Feminist Fables
Suniti Namjoshi

An ingenious reworking of fairytales. Mythology mixed with the
author's original material and vivid imagination. An indispensable
feminist classic.

Her imagination soars to breathtaking heights.
                              Kerry Lyon, *Australian Book Review*

ISBN 1-875559-19-1

St Suniti and the Dragon
Suniti Namjoshi

Ironic, fantastic, elegant and elegiac, fearful and funny. A
thoroughly modern fable.

*It's hilarious, witty, elegantly written, hugely inventive, fantastic,
energetic.*
                                                    U.A. Fanthorpe

ISBN: 1-875559-18-3

Building Babel
Suniti Namjoshi

A fabulous new book in which time, space and the discipline of love come under scrutiny.

Suniti Namjoshi is an inspired fabulist: she asks the difficult questions - about good and evil, about nature and war - unfailingly bracing her readers with her mordant humour and the lively play of her imagination.

Marina Warner

ISBN: 1-875559-56-6

Goja
Suniti Namjoshi

This powerful meditation, part autobiography, part elegy, deconstructs the glamour given to wealth and power and celebrates the quest for love.

ISBN 1-875559-97-3

Car Maintenance, Explosives and Love
and other contemporary lesbian writings
Susan Hawthorne, Cathie Dunsford and Susan Sayer (eds)

An anthology which explores the mechanics of daily life, the
explosiveness of relationships, and the geography of love.

ISBN 1-875559-62-0

Cowrie
Cathie Dunsford

*Cath Dunsford's first novel (of a series I hope) is a gentle,
determined, insightful and womanful book.*

Keri Hulme

*Cowrie is tightly woven, textured with colors, tastes and smells . . .
and definitely worth the read, so go bug your local bookstore.*

Fat Girl Magazine

ISBN: 1-875559-28-0

The Journey Home: Te Haerenga Kainga
Cathie Dunsford

This is lesbian fantasy dripping with luscious erotic imagery.

NZ Herald

ISBN 1-875559-54-X

Manawa Toa: Heart Warrior
Cathie Dunsford

Cowrie boards a ship bound for Moruroa Atoll during the French nuclear tests. As international attention increases, the stakes rise sharply. She is joined by Sahara, a young peace activist from England, and Marie-Louise, a French nuclear physicist. But can they be trusted? Can anyone be trusted?

ISBN: 1-875559-69-8

The Falling Woman
Susan Hawthorne

This is a beautiful book, written with powerful insight and captivating originality.

Julia Hancock, *Lesbians on the Loose*

ISBN: 1-875559-04-3

Bird
Susan Hawthorne

Many-eyed and many-lived is this poet, as seismologist or lover, bird or newborn child. To the classic figures of Sappho or Eurydice she brings all the Now! Here! sense of discovery that fires her modern girl taking lessons in flight.

Judith Rodriguez

ISBN: 1-875559-88-4

Figments of a Murder
Gillian Hanscombe

Babes is about lust. Babes is about power. But what else is she up to? Set in London, *Figments of a Murder* is passionate and satirical, probing images of self, sex, stardom and sisterhood.

ISBN: 1-875559-43-4

Sybil: The Glide of Her Tongue
Gillian Hanscombe

A book where the lesbian voice mediates the essential vitality of she dykes who have visions. A book where Gillian Hanscombe's poetry opens up meaning in such a way that it provides for beauty and awareness, for a space where one says yes to a lesbian we of awareness.

Nicole Brossard

ISBN: 1-875559-05-1

Imago
Francesca Rendle-Short

Imago is a story of love and obsession, of seduction and transformation. The threading together of skins and bodies.

ISBN: 1-875559-36-1

I Started Crying Monday
Laurene Kelly

Fourteen-year-old Julie starts crying on Monday when things go badly at school; worse is to come.

ISBN: 1-875559-78-7

*If you would like to know more about Spinifex Press
write for a free catalogue or visit our website*

SPINIFEX PRESS
PO Box 212 North Melbourne
Victoria 3051 Australia
<http://www.spinifexpress.com.au>